The Cocktail Keys

The Cocktail Keys

the six key classics that unlock the cocktail kingdom

Rob Cassels
Photography by Todd Antony

MURDOCH BOOKS

Contents

Introduction

If there was ever a golden age for cocktail making at home, it would have to be the 1950s. From Hollywood movies to Park Avenue advertising, the images from this era suggest that every household had its own cocktail bar and every occupant knew how to mix the perfect drink. Looking back from the vantage point of this new century, the repeated impression is one of young homeowners relaxing with a cocktail in hand, their lives enriched by newly affordable appliances. This image stands alongside the ill-fated hip of James Dean and the undiluted sex appeal of Marilyn Monroe as the quintessential symbols of 1950s chic. A large part of this impression is most likely myth, but judging by the sheer amount of cocktail paraphernalia that washes up in antique shops dating from that decade, there must be more than a grain of truth in it.

Recipes that have been etched down the sides of some of that antique cocktail equipment reveal the names of the drinks shaken and stirred by those 1950s households — the Manhattan, the White Lady, the Dry Martini. Familiar names to the modern-day cocktail aficionado and required learning for any aspiring bartender, but there was once a time when these classic recipes came close to extinction.

Antique stores can be fertile grounds for those hunting unique cocktail equipment.

The 1970s saw a new wave of cocktail design that swamped established drink-making principles. It was an era in which discos, flashing lights and bar blenders met in a whirl of thumping bass lines, flamboyant dance moves and Pina Coladas. Cocktails became taller, fruitier, creamier and fussier. Instead of accentuating the subtleties of the spirits used in their creation, recipes were invented to disguise the taste of (often cheap) base ingredients in order to encourage excessive (and profitable) consumption. Instead of simplicity, elegance or taste, these cocktails relied on gaudy trimmings — paper umbrellas and plastic sea horses — and titillating names like *Sex on the Beach* or *A Sloe Comfortable Screw* to sell themselves.

While these drinks sold in the millions, they were little more than alcoholic milkshakes and, as the craze wore off during the champagne-fuelled hedonism of the 1980s, it left the art of classic cocktail making on the verge of disappearing from mainstream culture.

Thankfully, a few obstinate drinking establishments refused to be submerged by the trendy drinking styles of the clubs and bars of the 1970s. Sticking to the principles upon which their drinks-mixing philosophy had originally been based, they dared to be different. While popular opinion saw these bars as old fashioned, they remained stubborn advocates of style and elegance over fad-fuelled popularity and still unrepentantly continued to mix *Old-Fashioneds* — the classics.

Some of those bars, including Harry's Bar in Paris, The American Bar at the Savoy in London, and the Rainbow Room in New York, are now legendary, as they helped fuel the cocktail renaissance of the 1990s. A rejuvenated bar industry inspired by those legends saw a new wave of retro cocktail lounges; while bartenders returned enthusiastically to the original recipes that had proved so popular and enduring in the 1950s. Based on these early principles of drink construction, innovative cocktail recipes emerged, driven by the classic formula of taste and sophistication rather than the gimmickry of the previous two decades. These fundamental rules, however, had to be prised from their original owners or dredged up from the vaults of cocktail history. Once these rules were obtained, the new owners were keen to give the impression that only they were privy to that vintage knowledge and they guarded their secrets

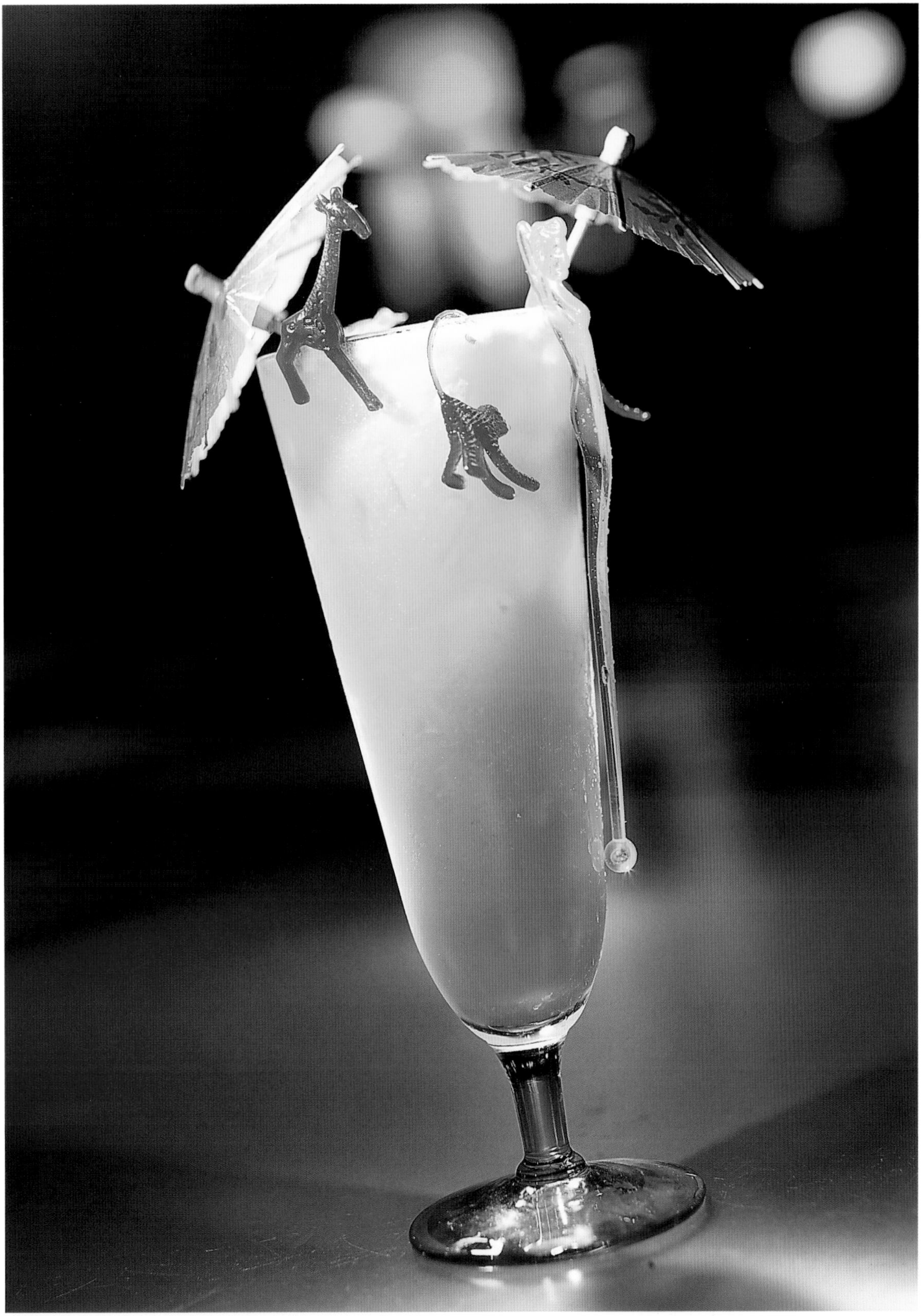

The Fluffy Duck — evil, orange and just plain wrong.

accordingly. The dexterity, flair and ritual of classic cocktail making, coupled with a new moniker — mixologist — merely added to the impression that elite skill and cocktail wisdom were required to mix and modify history's great drinks.

Today the bar industry still has a vested interest in maintaining the impression that only a dedicated professional has the tools and know-how to create classic cocktails. At some stage since the halcyon days of the classic home-made cocktail, the art of domestic drinks mixing appears to have been sadly forgotten.

That is not to say there are not thousands of cocktail books on the market, but they always seem to fall into two categories.

Firstly, there is the book for the bar professional. Often endorsed by a sage institute of bartending, this will claim to be *the* definitive collection of mixed drinks. It will then list, in exhaustive detail, a thousand or so cocktails while bearing a marked similiarity to the previous book that claimed to be the last word in cocktail making. Useful, perhaps, for the bartender suddenly faced with a customer demanding an obscure libation, but of little value to the home entertainer reluctant to invest in a vast range of little-used ingredients.

Then there is the book designed for the enthusiastic amateur. It will concentrate on one small area of cocktail making, such as martinis, yet still rely on the reader being able to obtain all the listed ingredients and slavishly follow each recipe to its exact measurements.

The aim of *The Cocktail Keys* is to introduce the reader to the six key cocktails that provide the basis for the vast majority of cocktail varieties enjoyed today. Instead of giving the exact measurements for ingredients, they are explained in terms of proportions. This allows the reader to tailor each recipe to suit the volume of their own glassware.

Once each key cocktail has been mastered, variations on each theme enable the home bartender to create thousands of original cocktail recipes while still retaining the fundamental principles that ensure each drink is simple, elegant and a classic in its own right.

The Mixologist may seem to hold arcane cocktail-making secrets but that knowledge is based on very simple principles.

Like any great cocktail, the Daiquiri has a story attached to it. Legend has it that two American mining engineers in eastern Cuba, Mr Pagliuchi and Mr Cox, found the local nightlife less than exhilarating. Seeking an alternative, they took the only local ingredients they could find — limes, sugar and Cuban rum — and created a smooth sweet–sour concoction that made life seem a lot less burdensome. Toasting their creation, they christened it the Daiquiri after the local mines.

What is known for certain is that the Daiquiri was refined and perfected by Ernest Hemingway's favourite bartender, Constante Ribalagua, at La Floridita Bar in downtown Havana. Known as *El Rey de los Coteleros* (The King of the Cocktails), Ribalagua is reputed to have made over 10 million Daiquiris during his 40 year career and, helped by the patronage of his famous customer, is responsible for turning that first simple recipe into the classic enjoyed today.

Legend aside, the importance of the Daiquiri is that it is the most basic unit of cocktail currency.

Like any great cocktail, the Daiquiri has a story attached to it. Legend has it that two American mining engineers in eastern Cuba, Mr Pagliuchi and Mr Cox, found the local nightlife less than exhilarating. Seeking an alternative, they took the only local ingredients they could find — limes, sugar and Cuban rum — and created a smooth sweet-sour concoction that made life seem a lot less burdensome. Toasting their creation, they christened it the Daiquiri after the local mines.

What is known for certain is that the Daiquiri was refined and perfected by Ernest Hemingway's favourite bartender, Constante Ribalagua, at La Floridita Bar in downtown Havana. Known as El Rey de los Coteleros (The King of the Cocktails), Ribalagua is reputed to have made over 10 million Daiquiris during his 40 year career and, helped by the patronage of his famous customer, is responsible for turning that first simple recipe into the classic enjoyed today.

Legend aside, the importance of the Daiquiri is that it is the most basic unit of cocktail currency.

The Daiquiri

The Daiquiri
3 parts Cuban white rum
1 part lime juice
1 ½ parts sugar syrup

Sweet and sour

As you can see, the Daiquiri is a simple mixture of a base spirit (rum) plus a sweet–sour combination using sugar syrup and fresh lime juice.

So, you might ask, what is all the fuss about?

The secret is in the combination of sweet and sour. When these two elements are perfectly balanced they mute the harsh alcoholic burn of a drink's spirit base while accentuating its hidden background flavours. Rather than simply adding flavours, the sugar and lime combination allows the drinker to taste the wonderful vanilla and caramel flavours found in the better brands of rum. A perfect Daiquiri is a beautifully restrained and subtle cocktail.

Creating exactly the right balance of sweet and sour is an essential element in the vast majority of the world's great classic cocktails. The key to making the perfect Daiquiri is to find exactly the point at which sweet balances sour. Too sour and the drink becomes undrinkable. Too sweet and, although perfectly palatable, the extra sugar hides the subtleties of the rum makers' art. Therefore, the first step in making a Daiquiri is to create the perfect balance of sweet and sour.

Making consistent sugar syrup is easy. The simplest method is to dissolve 1 kg (2 lb 4 oz/ 4⅓ cups) caster (superfine) sugar in 2 litres (70 fl oz/8 cups) boiling water and store in the refrigerator until required. The sugar syrup will give you a reliable sweetness, but the sour element from fresh citrus juice can often vary according to the ripeness of your fruit. Before making any drink with a sweet–sour balance at its heart, always test the juice first by combining a small amount of it with some sugar syrup to get just the right proportions for your mix. The mixture is perfectly balanced when your taste buds in charge of detecting sourness recognize it with just as much conviction as those detecting sweetness.

When you have exactly the right proportions of sweet and sour, combine with the rum, add to your shaker and shake vigorously for about 10 seconds, then immediately strain into a chilled glass.

As an alternative to shaking you can also try a technique known as flash blending. Flash blending is a method by which you can use your blender to mix a drink without overloading the final result with ice and watering down its taste. To flash blend, first add the cocktail ingredients and fill with enough ice to cover the blades of the blender. Blend with four or five short bursts of 2 seconds duration. Remove excess ice by straining the mixture into a chilled glass.

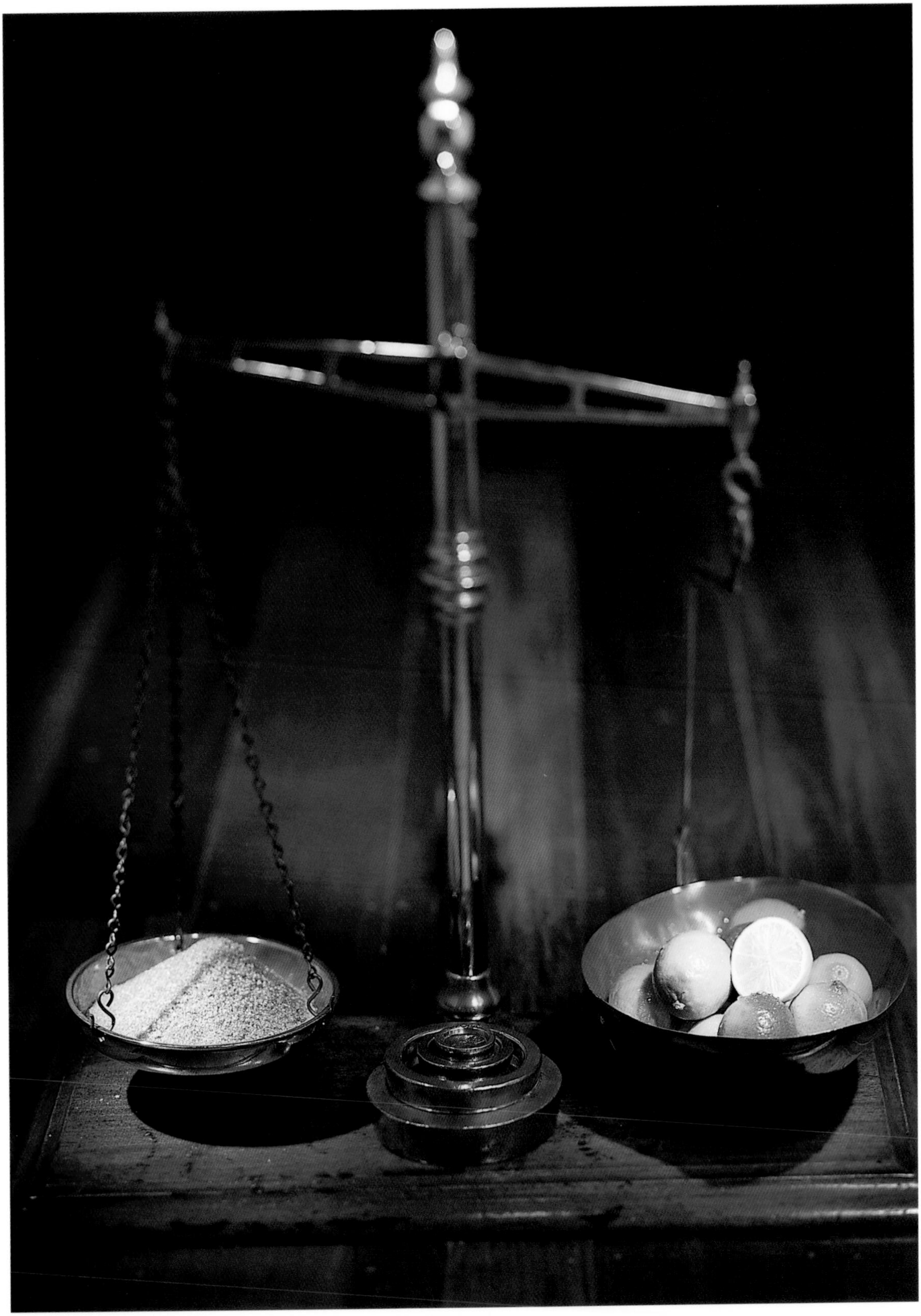

Accurate balancing of sweet and sour is essential.

Pineapple Daiquiri
3 parts Cuban white rum
1 part pineapple juice
$^{1}/_{2}$ part lime juice
1 part sugar syrup

Experimentation

Once you have mastered the basic, original Daiquiri, the door is open to experiment with this first key recipe by manipulating all three of the main ingredients.

Juices Firstly, try different juices. Lemon juice is an obvious substitute for lime but interesting combinations can also be found with either a sharp grapefruit or orange juice. Sweeter juices can be offset by the addition of smaller amounts of lime or lemon juice. Trying different combinations of juice together can also produce some delicious variations on the basic sweet–sour theme.

Pineapple juice can provide a worthwhile base from which to explore the world of the Daiquiri.

Bombay Sours
3 parts Bombay Sapphire gin
1 part lemon juice
1 1/2 parts sugar syrup

Spirits A simple way to create delicious new recipes is to experiment with different base spirits. Remember, the intention is to draw out the background flavours that are so painstakingly produced during the distilling process.

A casual sniff of a bottle, though, will seldom reveal those aromas as they are usually masked by the rather raw smell of alcohol. Instead, pour a few drops of your chosen spirit into the palm of your hand and briefly rub your palms together. The warmth of your hands will cause the majority of the alcohol to evaporate and will allow you to detect the more subtle flavours that your cocktail will highlight. Use this method with anejo rum, for example, which is aged in oak casks, and you will detect wonderfully complex scents of vanilla, cocoa, light tobacco and spices.

Try this technique with a variety of spirits. Not only will it reveal the underlying subtleties of the distiller's craft but it will also provide inspiration for further variations built around this basic recipe.

The citrus notes of Bombay Sapphire gin come from the lemon zest in botanicals added during the distilling process. This makes lemon juice a perfect match.

Pink Daiquiri
3 parts Cuban white rum
1 part lime juice
1 part grenadine

Sugar syrups Possibly the simplest way to vary your basic recipe is to vary the taste of your sugar syrup. There are a number of flavoured sugar syrups readily available from most alcohol suppliers. Grenadine, for example, is a sugar syrup made using pomegranates which not only adds a sweet flavour to any recipe that contains it, but also imparts a striking red colour. Take care when using other sugar syrups, however, as many of them are a great deal sweeter than home-made syrup and you will have to reduce the quantity used accordingly.

Experimenting with your own sugar syrups can also provide a simple and tasty alternative to a basic sugar syrup and allow you to match the nose of your base spirit with a syrup of your own design.

The delicate flavour of the Pink Daiquiri is a great example of what a basic sugar syrup substitution can do.

Vanilla Syrup

500 g (1 lb 2 oz/2¼ cups) sugar
1½ litres (52 fl oz/6 cups) water
2 vanilla pods, split

Vanilla syrup is an easy-to-make sugar syrup variation and has a long lifespan when kept in the refrigerator.

Warm the water in a saucepan and slowly bring to a simmer without boiling. Add the sugar and stir until dissolved. Add the split vanilla pods to the pan and simmer for 10 minutes. Remove the saucepan from the heat and allow to cool. Leaving the vanilla pods in the mixture, scrape the seeds into the liquid and chill in the refrigerator until you are ready to use it.

Fruit syrups are also easy to make. Simply substitute fruit for the vanilla pods in the above recipe and blend the mixture thoroughly before bottling.

Simple home-made syrups, such as vanilla, can often produce a more satisfying result than any ready-made sugar syrup.

Cuban Honey

3 parts Cuban anejo rum
1 part lime juice
1 part honey

Natural sugars It is also well worth experimenting with more natural sweeteners. Honey, in particular, comes in a number of styles and varieties and has a wonderfully complex taste that can complement your base spirit perfectly. Before adding honey to a shaker, add a dash of hot water to it and stir to make sure it has fully dissolved. This will ensure it can combine with the rest of your ingredients without sticking to the sides of your shaker.

The combination of honey with the rich taste of anejo rum turns the Daiquiri into a voluptuous Cuban Honey.

Golden Glove Daiquiri
3 parts Cuban white rum
1 part lime juice
1 ½ parts sugar syrup
¼ part Cointreau

Advanced experimentation

Alcoholic additions Having mastered and experimented with the three main elements of the Daiquiri, try further variations by making small additions to the basic three-ingredient mixture.

Remember, however, the lesson of simplicity that the Daiquiri teaches and beware the temptation to overcomplicate. We are looking to accentuate the subtleties contained in our chosen spirit by adding complementary flavours, rather than merely hiding the alcohol with a flood of extra tastes.

If we return to Constante Ribalagua for a moment, let's see how one of his original Daiquiri variations illustrates this point. In the Golden Glove Daiquiri, Ribalagua added a small amount of Cointreau, using the complex orange flavours to enhance the rum's deeper notes.

So, following the cocktail king's example, before flooding this simple drink with extra ingredients, make smaller additions based on what you have identified from the nose of your spirit base. A simple rule of thumb when modifying a Daiquiri with an alcoholic liqueur is to only use small quantities. If you think you haven't added enough, that is probably the perfect amount.

It may be hard for the palate to identify the small addition of Cointreau, but it alters the tone of the drink substantially.

Plum Daiquiri

3 parts Cuban white rum
1 part lime juice
$^1/_2$ part sugar syrup
1 part black plum flesh, mashed

Fruit additions Before going any further, let us look back to a snippet of cocktail history. After the 1959 Cuban revolution, the continuing evolution of the Daiquiri was left in the hands of bartenders in the United States. Unfortunately, this meant that when the 1970s transformed cocktail-drinking from a hallmark of sophistication into a demonstration of hedonism and excess, the Daiquiri was one of the drinks that became a standard bearer of the umbrella and sparkler movement.

The Daiquiri's downfall lay in its very simplicity. When blended with fruit, liqueur and large amounts of ice, the result was bland but inoffensive. This allowed bar owners to use small amounts of cheap spirits and survive in a competitive market. That is not to say there is no place for fruit in a Daiquiri — far from it. A perfectly made fruit Daiquiri can be one of the most satisfying cocktail experiences. Fruits that work best are those that have a tart quality to them or, if sweeter, can be highlighted by the addition of sour elements. While fresh fruit can produce great results, take care as the sweetness of fruit varies with its ripeness, affecting the balance of sweet and sour in the final mix.

Moving on The Daiquiri shows us how a simple recipe can be expanded into numerous variations. But what happens then when we substitute the non-alcoholic sweet element of that combination with a replacement containing alcohol? The answer lies with our next cocktail key — the Margarita.

The Plum Daiquiri is a deliciously tart summer Daiquiri alternative.

While there is little argument about the three basic ingredients that made up the first Margarita, the inventor's name remains hotly contested. Although the stories behind the Margarita's invention don't add anything to the flavour, they certainly increase the mystique surrounding this familiar cocktail.

The first story concerns Francisco 'Pancho' Morales, a bartender who was in a quandary when a customer ordered a cocktail called a Magnolia at his bar in Ciudad Juarez, Mexico, one night in 1942. Remembering only that it contained Cointreau, Morales added lime juice and tequila and liked the result so much he renamed his version the Margarita.

Alternatively, there is the 1938 claim of Carlos 'Danny' Herrera. He was asked for a drink by the fledgling actress Marjorie King who told him that, with the exception of tequila and Cointreau, she was allergic to alcohol. Using the Spanish version of her name, he named his solution to her problem the Margarita.

Most appealing perhaps, is the claim of Daniel Negrete who opened the Garci Crespo Hotel in Puebla, Mexico, with his brother David around 1934. On the day before his brother's wedding, Daniel presented David's bride-to-be with a new concoction made from tequila, lime juice and Cointreau to celebrate the occasion. Her name? Margarita.

Whatever the truth behind its inception might be, the Margarita has proved to be one of the world's great cocktails, an enduring classic and is the next of our cocktail keys.

While there is little argument about the three basic ingredients that made up the first Margarita, the inventor's name remains hotly contested. Although the stories behind the Margarita's invention don't add anything to the flavour, they certainly increase the mystique surrounding this familiar cocktail.

The first story concerns Francisco 'Pancho' Morales, a bartender who was in a quandary when a customer ordered a cocktail called a Magnolia at his bar in Ciudad Juarez, Mexico, one night in 1942. Remembering only that it contained Cointreau, Morales added lime juice and tequila and liked the result so much he renamed his version the Margarita.

Alternatively, there is the 1938 claim of Carlos 'Danny' Herrera. He was asked for a drink by the fledgling actress Marjorie King who told him that, with the exception of tequila and Cointreau, she was allergic to alcohol. Using the Spanish version of her name, he named his solution to her problem the Margarita.

Most appealing perhaps, is the claim of Daniel Negrete who opened the Garci Crespo Hotel in Puebla, Mexico, with his brother David around 1934. On the day before his brother's wedding, Daniel presented David's bride-to-be with a new concoction made from tequila, lime juice and Cointreau to celebrate the occasion. Her name? Margarita.

Whatever the truth behind its inception might be, the Margarita has proved to be one of the world's great cocktails, an enduring classic and is the next of our cocktail keys.

The Margarita

The Margarita
3 parts tequila blanco
1 part lime juice
1 part Cointreau

Like many cocktails, the proportions of the Margarita differ according to the taste of the individual drinker. The basic 3:1:1 recipe is an excellent base from which to find your own preference.

Margarita Royale
3 parts tequila blanco
1 part lime juice
1 part crème de cassis

Apple Margarita
3 parts tequila blanco
1 part lime juice
1 part sour apple liqueur

Technique

We will deal with the Margarita's salt rim later in the chapter but first let's look at how to mix the drink itself. As with the Daiquiri, the first step is to balance the sweet element of the drink, Cointreau, with the sour element, lime juice. Once your taste buds tell you that the mixture is perfectly balanced, add the tequila, then shake and serve.

A simple enough formula but instead of a basic sugar syrup, the sweetening agent here is Cointreau — an alcoholic liqueur made from a mixture of both sweet and bitter orange zest. This adds a wider range of flavours and additional alcohol to the recipe, giving an extra degree of depth and complexity to the taste of the Margarita.

Experimentation

Alcoholic liqueurs All alcoholic liqueurs differ in sweetness, alcoholic content and viscosity so be sure to test your proportions when substituting the Cointreau for another liqueur. That said, the wide range of flavoured liqueurs available on the market means it is easy to create a number of interesting variations on the basic theme of the Margarita by changing the liqueur base in the original recipe.

Margarita Royale (*left*) and Apple Margarita — two simple variations, two dramatically different results.

Frozen drinks There are few drink recipes that lend themselves well to being frozen. In general, blending a drink until it is 'frozen' means an enormous amount of ice is locked up with the other ingredients, thus watering down the cocktail and making for a rather wishy-washy result.

The Margarita is not necessarily an exception to this rule, but there is something about the robust nature of the taste of tequila that can survive the process a lot better than many other spirits. It's not recommended to make your Margaritas exclusively by this method, but it can prove to be an excellent option on a hot, sunny afternoon.

To make a thirst-quenching frozen Margarita, first put all the ingredients in a blender, add enough ice to just cover the blades and blend the mixure. Turn the blender off, add some more ice and blend again. Continue adding ice and blending until the desired consistency is reached. Spoon the mixture into chilled glasses.

There are times when you can get too carried away with the blender and decorations!

Frozen Strawberry Margarita
3 parts tequila blanco
1 part lime juice
1 part crème de fraise
3 parts strawberries

Fruit additions Given that almost all liqueurs are fruit-based, some of the best results involve the addition of fresh fruit ingredients combined with a matching liqueur. The Frozen Strawberry Margarita, for example, matches fresh strawberries with crème de fraise (strawberry liqueur).

If you avoid the temptation to overcomplicate the recipe by using too much fruit or making it too sweet, then you should achieve excellent results.

This Margarita proves that frozen drinks don't have to be naff — and can make a nice change from sorbet for dessert!

Blueberry Margarita
3 parts gold tequila
1 part lime juice
$^{1}/_{2}$ part cherry brandy
1$^{1}/_{2}$ parts blueberries

Once you have experimented with recipes containing liqueurs that match your fruit additions, you can start to look for combinations that complement each other.

In the recipe for the Blueberry Margarita, for example, cherry brandy is used to balance out the lime juice. The similarities between cherries and blueberries result in a deliciously integrated flavour.

The smoother tones of gold tequila add a beautiful, mellow depth to the Blueberry Margarita.

Apricot and Passionfruit Margarita

3 parts gold tequila
1 part lime juice
½ part apricot brandy
1 part passionfruit pulp

It isn't always necessary to try to match or find complementary flavours. A liqueur and fruit combination that appears to clash can sometimes produce wonderfully complex variations. Apricot brandy and passionfruit pulp illustrate this point perfectly and provide a number of subtle and interesting background tastes to the regular Margarita recipe.

Apricot and passionfruit are two contrasting flavours that combine to make a great unified whole.

Spirits Before experimenting with different spirits it is worth starting with the different varieties of tequila. Tequila is often derided and avoided by many, primarily because their first encounter was unpleasant. However, this can often be attributed to an overindulgence in a poor-quality spirit rather than a reflection on the tequila itself.

It might come as a surprise that tequila is subject to similar production rules to those that govern Cognac. While there are many brandies, only brandy made in the Cognac region of France can be so named. Likewise with the tequila-producing regions of Mexico. Only the spirit produced from the blue agave plant around the village of Tequila, and an additional area around Tepatitlan, can bear the name tequila. Although produced from the same plant, spirits made outside these areas are labelled mescal.

Before buying tequila, take some time finding a brand that is produced with a little more care than the standard fare, and the difference will be immediately apparent. There are four main types of tequila to look for: blanco (or silver) is clear in colour and has the most distinctive tequila strength and taste; gold is tequila blanco mellowed by the addition of caramel or other flavourings; reposado (rested) is tequila blanco that has been aged in white oak casks for between two months and one year, imparting a delicate golden colour and bouquet; and anejo (aged), which has been aged in white oak casks for over a year and develops a great subtlety and depth of flavour.

Mexican Cognac (*from left to right*): blanco, gold, reposado and anejo.

Top Shelf Margarita

3 parts tequila anejo
1 part lime juice
1 part Grand Marnier

Of course, any spirit can be substituted into the Margarita format with success and a great many very old and well-known cocktails are constructed on exactly the liqueur–juice–spirit principle we find in the Margarita.

As when experimenting with the Daiquiri, it is worth rubbing a few drops of your chosen spirit between the palms of your hands and then looking for a liqueur that matches the nose of the spirit.

The Top Shelf Margarita deserves a place among the cocktail aristocracy.

White Lady
3 parts gin
1 part lemon juice
1 part Cointreau

When following recipes, some of the older versions you may come across, like the original White Lady, call for egg white to be added to the shaker. While this produces a silkier feel on the tongue, the prevalence of salmonella in modern-day chicken production means that the use of raw egg is unadvisable.

As usual, the general rule of thumb is to keep the combinations as simple as possible. While experimenting with the aromas in your base spirits may tempt you to try using more than one as the base to a cocktail, it tends to overcomplicate the recipe and seldom produces good results.

Dating from the 1920s, the White Lady can rightly be judged one of the classics.

Salt rims Perhaps the most distinctive feature of the Margarita is the salt around the rim of the glass. The effect is to produce that wonderful salty hit on the lips with every mouthful, adding another element to tequila's unique flavour. Indeed, the purist would claim that without salt, the drink should no longer bear the name of Margarita.

Not all salts are created equal, however, and many table salts contain a number of added chemicals that prevent them from caking-up in damp conditions. Use a natural salt that contains no artificial additives. The uneven crystals of natural salt may require crushing but the difference in taste will become immediately apparent.

To create a salt rim, crush salt crystals and spread a thin layer on a flat surface. Holding the glass upside-down, rub the outside of the rim with a lime wedge and dip the glass in the salt.

The Flamingo
3 parts gin
1 part lime juice
1 part apricot brandy
¼ part grenadine

Sugar rims You needn't confine yourself to a salt rim on your glass. Sugar can be used instead and can be an effective way to not only provide a visually appealing garnish, but also to add extra zest to a simple recipe.

When rimming a glass with sugar you can also experiment by using coloured sugar syrups to dampen the rim of the glass. The Flamingo, for example, has a pink sugar rim, produced by wiping the edge of the glass with a sponge soaked in grenadine.

Experimenting with the liqueur–juice–spirit base of the Margarita and the rim of the glass should lead to a wide range of satisfying variations and it is worth spending some time investigating those before moving on to the next step.

Moving on But what is that next step? Following the premise that the soul of most classic cocktails is the central balance of sweet and sour, we have looked at juice–sugar and juice–liqueur combinations — so where do we go from here?

The answer lies with a drink that has been made in its home country for years but has only recently received worldwide recognition.

Our next cocktail key — the Caipirinha.

A coloured rim can add an extra visual element to your creations.

There are a number of things that seem to capture the essence of Brazil — the sensual rhythm of Samba, the fabled sands of Copacabana, sublimely skilful football and, it must be said, the Caipirinha.

The name stems from the word *caipara*, which can mean 'country people' politely or 'rednecks' less politely, and translates literally as 'little peasant girl'. The drink itself has been enjoyed by both rich and poor in Brazil for many years and the simple formula has long been recognized as Brazil's national drink.

During the 1990s, a newfound enthusiasm for the food, music and culture of South America, coupled with the global availability of cachaça — Caipirinha's main ingredient — led to a boom in the drink's popularity. As a result, the Caipirinha and its variants are some of the world's most requested cocktails.

At the heart of the Caipirinha's popularity lies a simple technique: muddling a fruit to release both its juice and the bitter essential oils contained in its skin.

There are a number of things that seem to capture the essence of Brazil — the sensual rhythm of Samba, the fabled sands of Copacabana, sublimely skilful football and, it must be said, the Caipirinha.

The name stems from the word caipara, which can mean 'country people', politely or 'rednecks', less politely, and translates literally as 'little peasant girl'. The drink itself has been enjoyed by both rich and poor in Brazil for many years and the simple formula has long been recognized as Brazil's national drink.

During the 1990s, a newfound enthusiasm for the food, music and culture of South America, coupled with the global availability of cachaca — Caipirinha's main ingredient — led to a boom in the drink's popularity. As a result, the Caipirinha and its variants are some of the world's most requested cocktails.

At the heart of the Caipirinha's popularity lies a simple technique: muddling a fruit to release both its juice and the bitter essential oils contained in its skin.

The Caipirinha

The Caipirinha
3 parts cachaça
1 lime, cut into 6 wedges, per glass
2 teaspoons raw (demerara) sugar per glass
crushed ice

Despite its simplicity and allegedly humble origins, the Caipirinha is a wonderfully complex and satisfying drink.

The basics

Cachaça Legend has it that cachaça ('ka-shah-sah') was first concocted by slaves working on sugar-cane plantations who drank the crop's fermented juice. Cachaça is manufactured in a similar way to rum except that it is fermented and distilled from pure sugar cane juice rather than molasses — the by-product of sugar cane. Whatever its origins, there are now at least 4000 brands of cachaça ranging from the basic raw spirit to smooth, oak-aged varieties. Cachaça is known by dozens of synonyms ranging from *purinha* (little pure one) to *engaga gato* (cat choker), depending on the region in which it is produced and the quality of the finished product. It is important, therefore, to discover at which end of that scale a bottle of cachaça lies before purchasing it.

Muddler A muddler is a wooden pestle, which is used to mash the lime and sugar in a Caipirinha. If you don't have either a muddler or a traditional pestle then the back of a large spoon can still be used to good effect.

Mixing technique To mix the basic Caipirinha, take a large, sturdy glass. Muddle the lime wedges and sugar together with a downward twisting motion. Immediately you will notice a sharp citrus zest smell as the oils contained in the lime zest are expelled. Don't be afraid to use a degree of force; it is important to make sure that as much as possible of the fruit's juice is released to combine with the sugar, making the all-important sweet and sour combination.

When you are satisfied that all the sugar has dissolved, cover the mixture with crushed ice, pressing it down gently with the palm of your hand to make sure the glass is packed full. Then top with cachaça, stir through and serve.

The importance of this technique is that here, unlike drinks that use squeezed juice, the oils from the zest of the fruit are incorporated into the sweet–sour combination, adding yet another layer of subtlety to the finished result. In the case of the Caipirinha, for example, the essential oils of the lime contribute a sharpness that both refreshes and stimulates the taste buds.

The popularity of the Caipirinha has now spawned a whole family of drinks, known as 'stick drinks', which are based on the muddling technique. Before we look at how to expand on this method, however, let us take another quick look at ice — one of our most important ingredients.

A simple way to make sweet and sour but it is the addition of the lime's zesty oils that makes muddling such a useful technique.

Crushed ice As discussed earlier, the importance of good, fresh ice is often overlooked when it comes to cocktail making. Nowhere is it more important to have good-quality frozen water than when you are filling drinks with crushed ice.

Crushed ice has a much larger surface area than the equivalent amount of cubed ice and will therefore melt much faster. If you use ice made from tap water, a number of chemicals the water contains, such as fluoride, will gradually be introduced into the finished product and affect the flavour. Even the most basic, store-bought ice will be made from water that has been filtered prior to freezing. So, at the very least, have a supply of store-bought ice on hand but preferably, make your own from spring water or find a local supplier of superior quality ice.

When it comes to crushing ice, there are many hand-powered ice crushers available on the market, but even without one crushed ice is easy to prepare. The simplest method of crushing ice is to wrap it tightly in a clean tea towel (dish cloth) and beat it with a mallet or rolling pin on a firm surface. To keep the crushed ice handy, you can leave it in a sieve to allow it to drain.

Drinks are seldom served 'frappé' after modern dinner parties, but the simple addition of crushed ice to a favourite liqueur can make a delicious digestif.

Gin Daisy
6 parts gin
2 parts lemon juice
1 part grenadine
crushed ice

Few modern cocktail recipes call for the use of crushed ice, but some great results can be achieved by straining your creations into a glassful. Many of the older classic cocktails were created with crushed ice in mind and, while their names may seem outdated, the principles upon which they are based are timeless.

The Gin Daisy is a simple Gin Sours which substitutes grenadine for sugar syrup and is served on crushed ice.

Margarita Stick Drink

3 parts tequila blanco
1 lime, cut into 6 wedges, per glass
1 part Cointreau
pinch of sea salt
crushed ice

Stick drinks

The combination of the oils from a fruit's zest combined with its juice can dramatically change the overall taste of a drink. Let us look at how it can change the previous cocktail key, the Margarita. In this case, we replace the raw (demerara) sugar and muddle the lime wedges with a liqueur instead — Cointreau. Bear in mind that many liqueurs are made using a base of extracted oils from the zest of a fruit. The flavour from the combination of the orange oils in the Cointreau plus the oils from the fresh limes adds an extra contrasting layer of taste to the basic Margarita. In addition, a pinch of salt to the mixture can provide a tasty edge.

Muddling adds a sublime zest to the traditional Margarita.

Mango Caipirinha
3 parts cachaça
1 lime, cut into 6 wedges, per glass
1 teaspoon raw (demerara) sugar per glass
1 tablespoon mango flesh per glass
crushed ice

Apart from the fact that muddling releases the essential oils from a fruit's zest, one of the reasons stick drinks have become so popular is that the process enables the cocktail maker to add and mash other fruits without having to rely on a blender.

Excellent results can be obtained by adding slices of fresh fruit to the Caipirinha mixture before muddling. Again, don't be shy about muddling the mixture quite forcefully — it is important that the fruit has thoroughly combined with the other ingredients.

As with the Daiquiri, it is best to use good-quality fruit at the correct ripeness but, if availability is limited, tinned or frozen fruit can produce some equally pleasing results.

The deliciously sweet, syrupy mango taste combines perfectly with the sharp tang of limes to make a truly fabulous fruit Caipirinha.

Orange Caipiroska

3 parts vodka
$\frac{1}{2}$ orange, cut into 3 wedges, per glass
2 teaspoons raw (demerara) sugar per glass
crushed ice

Lemon Caipiroska

3 parts vodka
$\frac{1}{2}$ lemon, cut into 3 wedges, per glass
2 teaspoons raw (demerara) sugar per glass
crushed ice

Further experimentation Once you have mastered the art of muddling, experiment with other stick drinks using different spirits, sugar syrups and fruit liqueurs.

As with all the cocktail keys, remember that you are trying to match a set of different tastes that work together to create a combined whole. A good starting point would be to use other citrus fruits.

Substitute vodka for cachaça and the Caipirinha becomes a Caipiroska. These simple orange and lemon variants demonstrate the delicious versatility of the basic muddling formula.

Honey Caipirinha

3 parts cachaça
1 lime, cut into 6 wedges, per glass
2 teaspoons honey per glass
crushed ice

As with the first cocktail key, the Daiquiri, some of the most creative and delicious variations develop through experimenting with different sugars and sugar syrups. Again, the rule of thumb is to try to find combinations that work well together.

A simple honey addition makes a wonderfully smooth Caipirinha.

Brandy Hot Toddy
3 parts brandy
1 lemon, cut into 6 wedges, per glass
2 teaspoons honey per glass
top with boiling water

Muddling does not have to be confined to producing cold drinks. Deliciously soothing hot drinks are easy to create as a tasty bedtime alternative to cocoa, or when a medicinal winter pick-me-up is required. Simply muddle your chosen ingredients in a mug or coffee glass, top with boiling water and stir through.

While there are as many recipes for Hot Toddy as there are for Punch, the general rule is the simpler, the better.

Passionfruit Caipirinha
3 parts cachaça
1 lime, cut into 6 wedges, per glass
1 teaspoons raw (demerara) sugar per glass
2 teaspoons passionfruit pulp per glass

Further techniques As discussed earlier, one disadvantage of using crushed ice is the rapid rate at which it melts. This means your drink will become increasingly weaker the longer it sits untouched.

One way to combat this is to use pre-chilled glasses — something that is preferable with all cocktail making but sometimes impractical given limited refrigerator space. Another is to use whole ice cubes in your Caipirinhas instead of crushed ice. This does mean, however, that the cachaça element can end up being overwhelmingly strong and many of the drink's subtleties can be lost.

An excellent alternative, and one that ensures a well-chilled, well-balanced mix, is to use a technique termed the 'shake and dump'. Simply muddle the ingredients in the bottom half of a shaker. Add whole ice cubes, shake and then dump the entire contents into your glass. Shaking and dumping performs three tasks: it chills the drink thoroughly while still causing a small degree of melting during the shaking process, preventing the spirit base from being too overpowering; it ensures the components are completely combined — making a uniform and even drink from first to last sip; and it also punches air into the mixture, leaving the finished product with an attractive and tasty froth.

Shaking and dumping the Passionfruit Caipirinha ensures that the tangy sweetness of the passionfruit pulp invades every part of the finished mix.

Pina Caipirinha
3 parts cachaça
1 lime, cut into 6 wedges, per glass
2 teaspoons raw (demerara) sugar per glass
1 tablespoon pineapple flesh per glass
top with pineapple juice

Longer drinks The shake-and-dump technique also enables you to turn the basic Caipirinha into a longer drink by simply adding juice. Add the extra juice before shaking the ingredients to make sure you achieve an even mixture, and then dump into a tall glass. If you are using a Boston shaker (see page 164), the drink could be served in the glass half of the shaker.

The pineapple variant of the Caipirinha becomes a tropical thirst quencher by simply adding juice.

Bloody Mary Deluxe
3 parts vodka
2 lemon wedges per glass
worcestershire sauce, to taste
Tabasco sauce, to taste
celery salt, to taste
freshly ground black pepper, to taste
top with tomato juice

Even the humblest mixture can be improved by turning it into a stick drink. The everyday Bloody Mary, for example, is simply a spiced tomato juice spiked with vodka. However, by muddling the lemon wedges with the vodka beforehand, then shaking and dumping with the spiced mixture, this traditional recipe is transformed into something far superior.

Moving on Now that we have looked at a number of variations based on shorter drinks, let's look at how we might experiment with a taller recipe. Probably the simplest recipe for a tall drink would be one that has a spirit base balanced with the sweet–sour combination and topped with a sparkling water.

The recipe we will look at is the oldest of our cocktail keys — the Tom Collins.

The Bloody Mary Deluxe turns a good, basic drink into the ultimate 'morning-after' nourisher.

According to many cocktail histories, the Tom Collins — a tall, refreshing mixture of lemon juice, sugar, gin and soda water — was originally called a John Collins. The stories tell of a bartender called John Collins, at the long departed Limmer's Hotel in London, who mixed the self-titled original and the formula was only called a Tom Collins when made with a sweetened gin sold under the label of Old Tom. Eventually, irrespective of the gin used, the Tom Collins became the more familiar title and John Collins' claim on the formula slipped into cocktail obscurity.

One thing that is for certain is that the recipe dates from at least the tail end of the nineteenth century, ranking it among the world's first cocktails. This makes this simple unit of spirit, sweet and sour, topped with soda, the most venerable of our cocktail keys.

According to many cocktail histories, the Tom Collins — a tall, refreshing mixture of lemon juice, sugar, gin and soda water — was originally called a John Collins. The stories tell of a bartender called John Collins, at the long departed Limmer's Hotel in London, who mixed the self-titled original and the formula was only called a Tom Collins when made with a sweetened gin sold under the label of Old Tom. Eventually, irrespective of the gin used, the Tom Collins became the more familiar title and John Collins' claim on the formula slipped into cocktail obscurity.

One thing that is for certain is that the recipe dates from at least the tail end of the nineteenth century, ranking it among the world's first cocktails. This makes this simple unit of spirit, sweet and sour, topped with soda, the most venerable of our cocktail keys.

The Tom Collins

The Tom Collins
3 parts gin
1 part lemon juice
1 ^{1}/$_2$ parts sugar syrup
top with soda water

Elegant and refined, the Tom Collins has refreshed thirsty guests for well over a century.

Building drinks

The reason the Tom Collins has survived for well over a century is that it relies on a simple, winning formula that may seem familiar from our first cocktail key, the Daiquiri. The Tom Collins is the same basic unit of spirit with sweet and sour as the Daiquiri, but this time is topped with soda. This makes it the perfect base from which to develop and experiment with further recipes. Unlike the Daiquiri, however, the Tom Collins does not require either a blender or a shaker. Instead the drink is mixed together by a method known as 'building'.

First, create the all-important sweet–sour base with the lemon juice and sugar syrup. Then, simply add to an ice-filled tall glass, combine with the gin of your choice and top with soda water while stirring briskly.

The Collins family The Collins recipe is a great way to serve spirits and, given that lemon, sugar and soda make a fresh and preservative-free lemonade, can often be a real improvement on drinking spirits with canned or bottled sodas. An obvious place to begin experimenting with the Tom Collins, therefore, would be to vary the base spirit. Given the age of the original recipe, however, it will come as no surprise that there have been others through the years who have experimented with the substitution of the gin base and aptly named the variations.

The Collins family — Pierre Collins (Cognac), Colonel Collins (bourbon), Ivan Collins (vodka), Sandy Collins (scotch whiskey) and Pedro Collins (dark rum).

Bloody Campari Collins
3 parts Campari
2 parts blood orange juice
$\frac{1}{2}$ part sugar syrup
top with soda water

Despite their age, and the slightly old-fashioned titles, all of the Collins variations are well worth trying and, with a bottle of pre-mixed sweet and sour and a bottle of soda water, can be some of the simplest cocktails to prepare. Your experimentation with the Collins, though, needn't be confined to simply varying the spirit base. As with all the cocktail keys, the most delicious modifications come from balancing different, yet complementary, flavours.

These flavours do not come just from spirits. Many aperitifs such as Pernod or Dubonnet, for example, are best served as tall drinks and work really well using the Collins blueprint. Campari also thrives as a component of the Collins. The Bloody Campari Collins simply substitutes Campari for the gin and blood oranges for the lemons of the original recipe.

The Bloody Campari Collins fuses the wonderful raspberry-orange flavour of blood oranges with the distinctive bittersweet aperitif, Campari.

Moscow Mule Deluxe
3 parts vodka
$\frac{1}{2}$ part lime juice
$\frac{1}{2}$ part Cointreau
top with ginger beer

The fundamentals of the Collins can also help when giving existing recipes a refreshing overhaul. For example, let us look at how to update that simple (but slightly bland) vodka and ginger beer standard — the Moscow Mule.

Firstly, the sweet and sour balance: orange and lime combine well with ginger so let us make the heart of our new Mule from that of the Margarita — Cointreau and lime juice — but only use a small amount to keep its effect in the background.

Then, with the simple addition of vodka plus a good-quality ginger beer (good ginger beer *must* contain sediment) the Moscow Mule is transformed into something far more sublime.

A simple manipulation of a standard formula turns the Moscow Mule into a world class cocktail.

Gin Fizz

3 parts gin
1 part lemon juice
1 ½ parts sugar syrup
top with soda water

The Fizz One simple, yet effective, way to add another element to the Collins is to shake the ingredients before adding the soda water. Again, history has dictated that we are following in the footsteps of previous explorers but this technique, which transformed the Tom Collins into the Gin Fizz some 120 years ago, can open the gates to some superb variations.

What this shaking process does is pump a mass of tiny air bubbles into the mixture before you add the soda, resulting in a gloriously frothy head to the finished drink. The effect of those bubbles is that, apart from the froth, the flavours at the heart of the drink become refreshingly enhanced. Take care to add the soda water slowly — if added too quickly, the Fizz can easily froth over and out of the glass.

By changing the four base elements of sparkling, sweet, sour and spirit, the creative possibilities on this theme are virtually endless.

A vintage recipe that offers a number of modern possibilities.

Absinthe Fizz
3 parts absinthe
1 part lemon juice
1 ½ parts sugar syrup
top with soda water

Before being sidetracked by the more extravagant possibilities of the Fizz, it is well worth trying alternatives to the more usual spirits.

Absinthe, for example, is only recently making a comeback, having been banned in most countries for many years due to the psychoactive properties of one of its ingredients — wormwood. Modern varieties have now cut down on the amount of wormwood used, but lurid tales from absinthe's past have ensured its cult status. Modern drinkers will often drink absinthe as a shot, but in the past it was more usually imbibed with water. It proves to be an excellent candidate for conversion into a Fizz.

Once the scourge of French painters, absinthe is making a comeback.

Pineapple Fizz

3 parts white rum
1 part pineapple juice
¹/₂ part lime juice
¹/₂ part sugar syrup
top with dry ginger ale

Obviously, as with the Collins, we do not need to be inhibited by using only soda water as our carbonated element. From what we have learned from the other cocktail keys, we can experiment with confidence, knowing the elements that will work in one case will work in another.

The Pineapple Fizz, for example, is a simple variation on the Pineapple Daiquiri found in the Daiquiri chapter. Using that recipe as a base, we can develop it into a Fizz of our own creation by adding dry ginger ale.

Pineapple juice coupled with the bite of dry ginger ale, makes the Pineapple Fizz a delicious tropical thirst quencher.

Diamond Fizz
3 parts gin
1 part lemon juice
1 ½ parts sugar syrup
top with méthode champenoise

Champagne cocktails It is impossible to experiment with the Fizz without being tempted to add the ultimate sparkling element — Champagne. There is something decidedly decadent and sophisticated about great Champagne cocktails but, before getting carried away, it is worth remembering a point about ingredients.

While it is important to use the best ingredients you can find for making cocktails, the same does not necessarily apply to Champagne cocktails. Great Champagne is not made in huge quantities and as such, is always expensive. It is also made with the intention of being enjoyed unadulterated and is an exceptional drink on its own. Conversely, bad Champagne can be a tired and shabby brew and is not worth using at all.

There are, however, a number of excellent-quality méthode champenoises produced throughout the world that are often far better than most of the lowliest French Champagnes. They are also available at a price that allows them to be used in your cocktails without breaking the bank. When looking for a méthode, remember that the drier varieties tend to produce better cocktails than the sweeter ones.

So, setting aside any quibbles about whether these should be titled Méthode Champenoise Cocktails, let us first look at the Champagne version of the Gin Fizz — the Diamond Fizz.

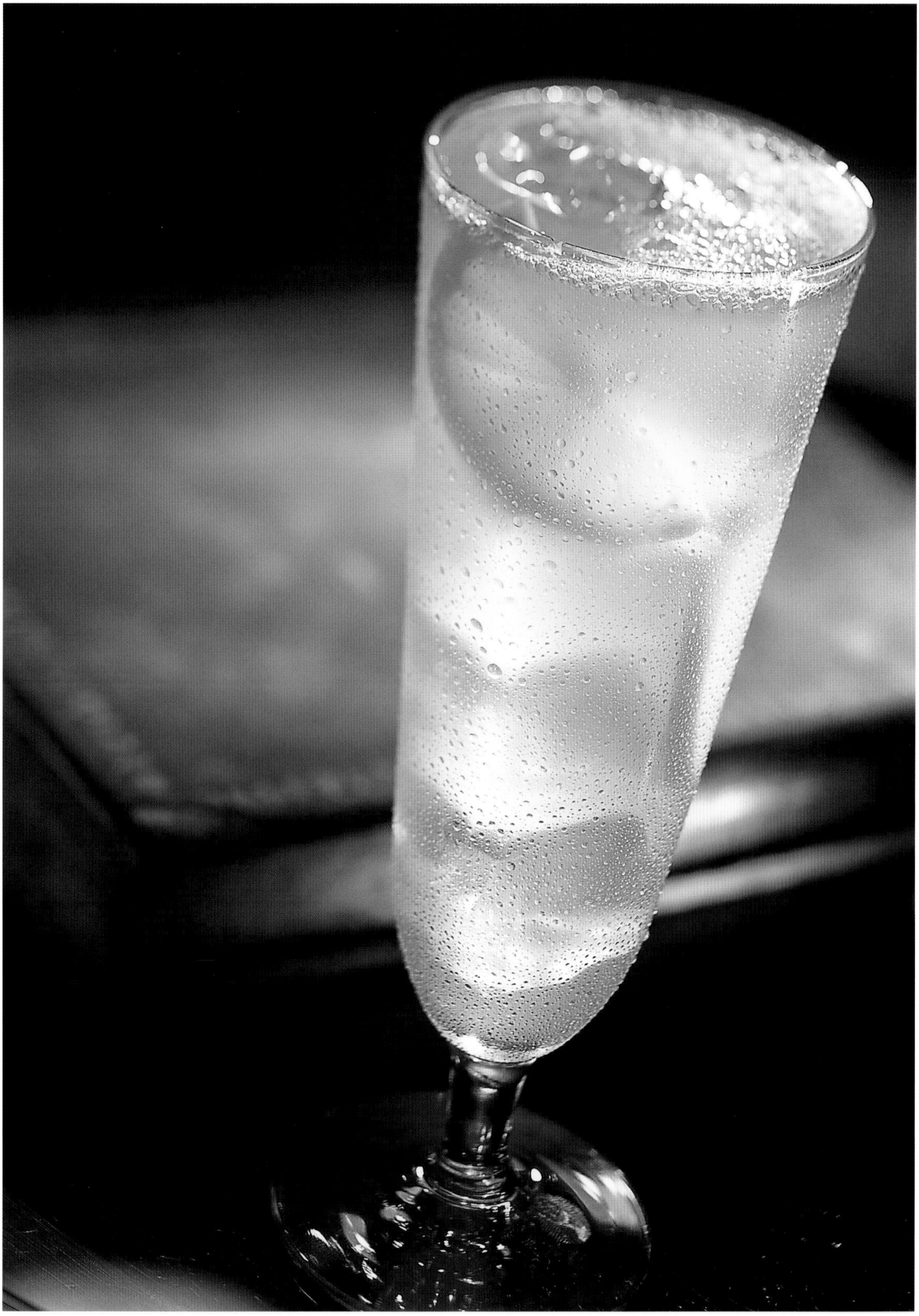

A bubbling upgrade to the standard Gin Fizz.

Kir Imperial
8 parts méthode champenoise
1 part crème de framboise

Simply substituting Champagne for the soda water in the Gin Fizz recipe produces mixed results. In the Gin Fizz, the soda water is used to lengthen the drink while maintaining the taste balance. It works because soda water has a relatively neutral taste but this is not true of méthode champenoise, which is much more complex. So, with the Diamond Fizz, the gin, sugar and lemon juice element is better employed highlighting the tastes in the bubbly. Dropping the amount of those elements until they constitute a quarter of the finished cocktail will produce much better results.

While the Diamond Fizz is served in a tall glass, more often than not Champagne cocktails are for occasions that call for elegant and stylish refreshments and for this reason are far more aesthetically pleasing when served in a Champagne flute.

Simple liqueur additions can be the key to the best Champagne cocktails. It is best to taste your choice of bubbly first and then use a liqueur that will complement its flavours. The Kir Imperial, for example, uses crème de framboise to add subtle sweetness and a delicate rose tint.

A touch of framboise makes one of the great Champagne cocktails.

French '75'
2 parts Cognac
$^{1}/_{2}$ part lemon juice
$^{1}/_{2}$ part sugar syrup
9 parts méthode champenoise

Spirits can be used in Champagne cocktails but take care, as the extra alcohol can easily swamp the more fragile flavours of the sparkling wine. The best way to incorporate a spirit base is to mute that extra alcohol and, as we know, one of the most effective methods of doing that is to introduce a sweet–sour balance to the mixture. Let us look at a vintage cocktail, the French '75', to see how it works.

The French '75' was allegedly invented at Harry's Bar, Paris, during World War 1 and was named after a French artillery piece. Like many drinks from that era, there is some disagreement as to the original ingredients and some have the spirit base as Cognac while others claim it as gin. Cognac is perhaps the most likely, given that it was far more commonly available in France during that period.

Sugar and lemon juice provide the central sweet and sour element, allowing the Cognac, a distillation of fermented grapes, to combine well with the méthode champenoise.

Moving on Having looked at the Tom Collins, one of the oldest drinks in the cocktail world, let us move on to a recipe which uses a technique that has only become popular in recent years. This method involves using the muddler to obtain the fragrant oils from herbs and the recipe is the next of our cocktail keys — the Mojito.

Both gin and Cognac versions of this venerable cocktail are well worth trying.

Thanks to the patronage of Constante Ribalagua's most famous customer, Ernest Hemingway, the Daiquiri served at El Floridita Bar was imitated around the cocktail world from the 1930s until the present day. The great writer's other favourite Cuban tipple, the Mojito, from Havana's Bodeguita Del Medio, had to wait a few years, however, before it received the same degree of popularity. It wasn't until the 1990s, and the wave of Latin chic that also saw the rise of the Caipirinha that the Mojito acquired global popularity and became an essential part of every bartender's repertoire.

The secret to the Mojito's delicate minted taste is, of course, the aromatic oils contained in mint leaves, and the technique of extracting these oils by gentle muddling.

Thanks to the patronage of Constante Ribalagua's most famous customer, Ernest Hemingway, the Daiquiri served at El Floridita Bar was imitated around the cocktail world from the 1930s until the present day. The great writer's other favourite Cuban tipple, the Mojito, from Havana's Bodeguita Del Medio, had to wait a few years, however, before it received the same degree of popularity. It wasn't until the 1990s, and the wave of Latin chic that also saw the rise of the Caipirinha that the Mojito acquired global popularity and became an essential part of every bartender's repertoire.

The secret to the Mojito's delicate minted taste is, of course, the aromatic oils contained in mint leaves, and the technique of extracting these oils by gentle muddling.

The Mojito

The Mojito
5 parts white rum
1 part lime juice
1 ½ parts sugar syrup
5 mint leaves per glass
top with soda water

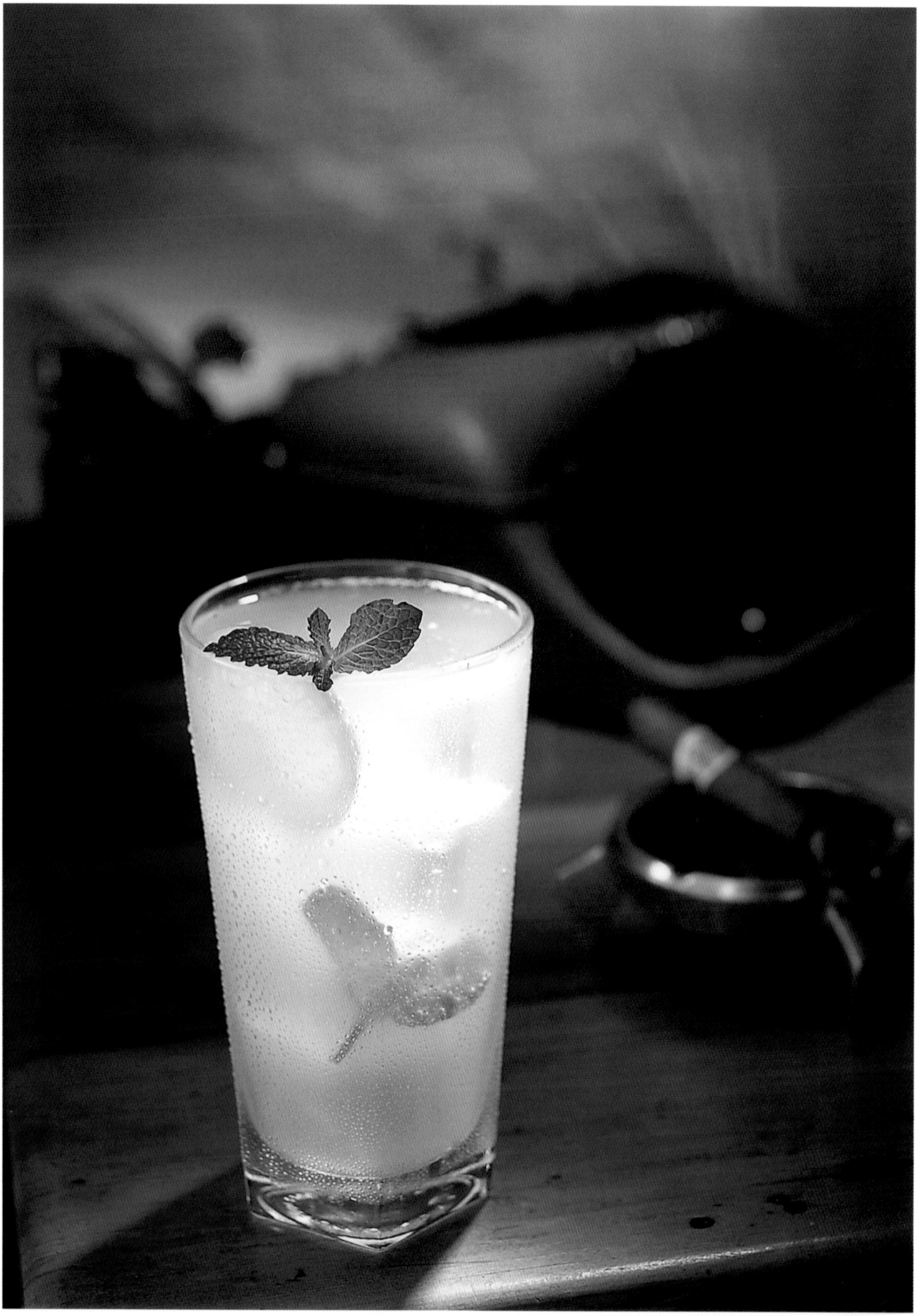

The newly chic Mojito has a classic Cuban background.

Technique

Before we launch ourselves into making the Mojito, it is worth remembering the lessons learned from our first cocktail key, the Daiquiri. As we can see from the main ingredients, the Mojito is essentially a minted Daiquiri topped with soda water. In the case of the Mojito, particular care should be taken to exactly balance the sugar and lime juice, or the delicate flavours from the mint will be almost entirely lost to the palate. Once you have muddled the mint in your glass, remove it, add the lime juice, rum and ice and top with soda water while stirring thoroughly. Finally garnish the Mojito with fresh mint and serve.

Given the clean, refreshing taste of the Mojito, it is remarkable that many early cocktails featuring mint had been sadly neglected until relatively recently. The exception is, of course, the Mint Julep.

Take care to muddle mint gently. If you crush the leaves too hard, the leaves' bitter juices will be released.

Mint Julep

4 parts rye whiskey

1 part sugar syrup

5 mint leaves per glass

Angostura bitters, to taste

crushed ice

Juleps

While the Mint Julep has always been synonymous with the Kentucky Derby, its origins actually pre-date the first running of the famous race in 1875, with some recipes dating from as early as 1815. Given its age, it is hardly surprising that the Mint Julep probably boasts as many 'definitive' recipes as there have been horses who have made it to the winner's enclosure.

That said, the basic Mint Julep is very simple to make.

Gently muddle the sprigs of mint in your mixing glass with the sugar syrup and bitters. Once muddled, remove the used leaves, add the rye whiskey and stir. Then strain the mixture into a chilled glass or frosted tankard that has been packed with crushed ice. Finally, garnish the finished Julep with a sprig of fresh mint.

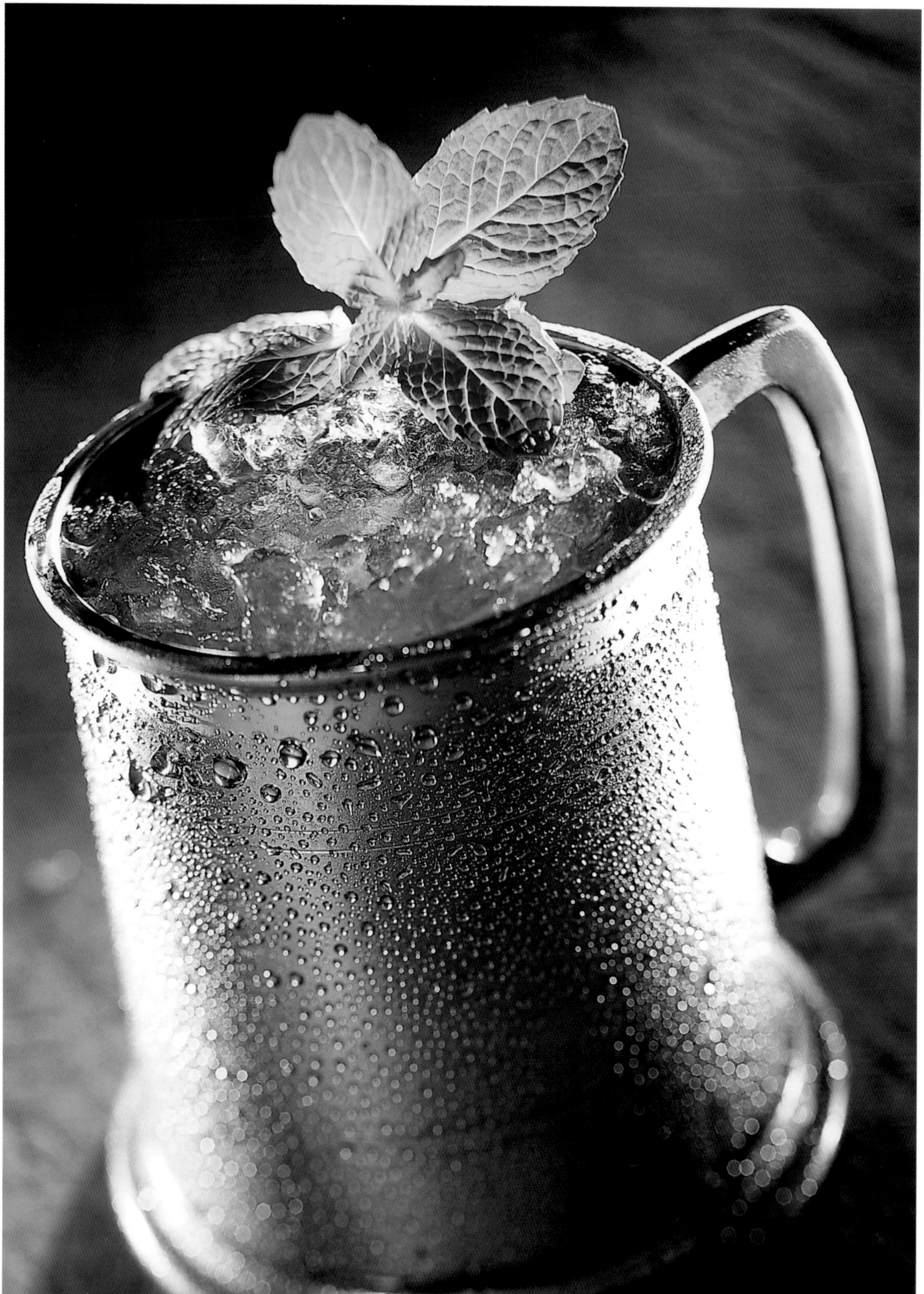

The ideal accompaniment to the big race.

Southern Comfort Julep
4 parts Southern Comfort
1/2 part sugar syrup
5 mint leaves per glass
Angostura bitters, to taste

The basic Mint Julep recipe can spawn some delicious variations and it's worth trying this formula with a variety of different spirit bases. Southern Comfort, for example, is a peach-flavoured bourbon and can provide a tasty alternative to rye whiskey.

Although the Julep is always best served by using fresh mint, if you are making large quantities it is possible to prepare minted sugar syrup in advance to avoid the need for repetitive muddling. Follow the vanilla sugar syrup recipe from page 24 and substitute a large bunch of shredded mint for the vanilla pods. When the mixture has cooled, strain, bottle and keep in the refrigerator until required.

The sweetness of Southern Comfort means this refreshing Julep requires less sugar.

Brandy Smash
5 parts brandy
1 part sugar syrup
5 mint leaves per glass
crushed ice

Experimentation

While a number of modern recipes now omit Angostura bitters from the Mint Julep, the original name for this variation was actually known as the Smash. A simple mix of mint, sugar and spirit, the Smash could be regarded as Mojito's simpler cousin, so let's look at the Smash recipe and then add further layers of complexity.

A Brandy Smash is made almost exactly the same way as our basic Julep. Add the sprigs of mint to your mixing glass together with the sugar syrup. Gently muddle the mint and sugar together and then add the brandy. Remove the mint, pour the mixture into a shaker, shake and serve over crushed ice.

The Brandy Smash is a minted, sweet concoction worthy of resurrection.

Vodka International
5 parts vodka
1 part lime juice
1 ½ parts sugar syrup
5 mint leaves per glass

Let's now add a sour element and look at the results. Once again, we can take our lead from the earlier cocktail keys. If we substitute vodka for the rum in a Daiquiri, and muddle mint into the sugar syrup before shaking, a Daiquiri becomes the outstanding Vodka International.

The Vodka International shows the fantastic results that can be produced by infusing mint into the simplest of recipes and provides fertile ground for experimentation with other spirit bases.

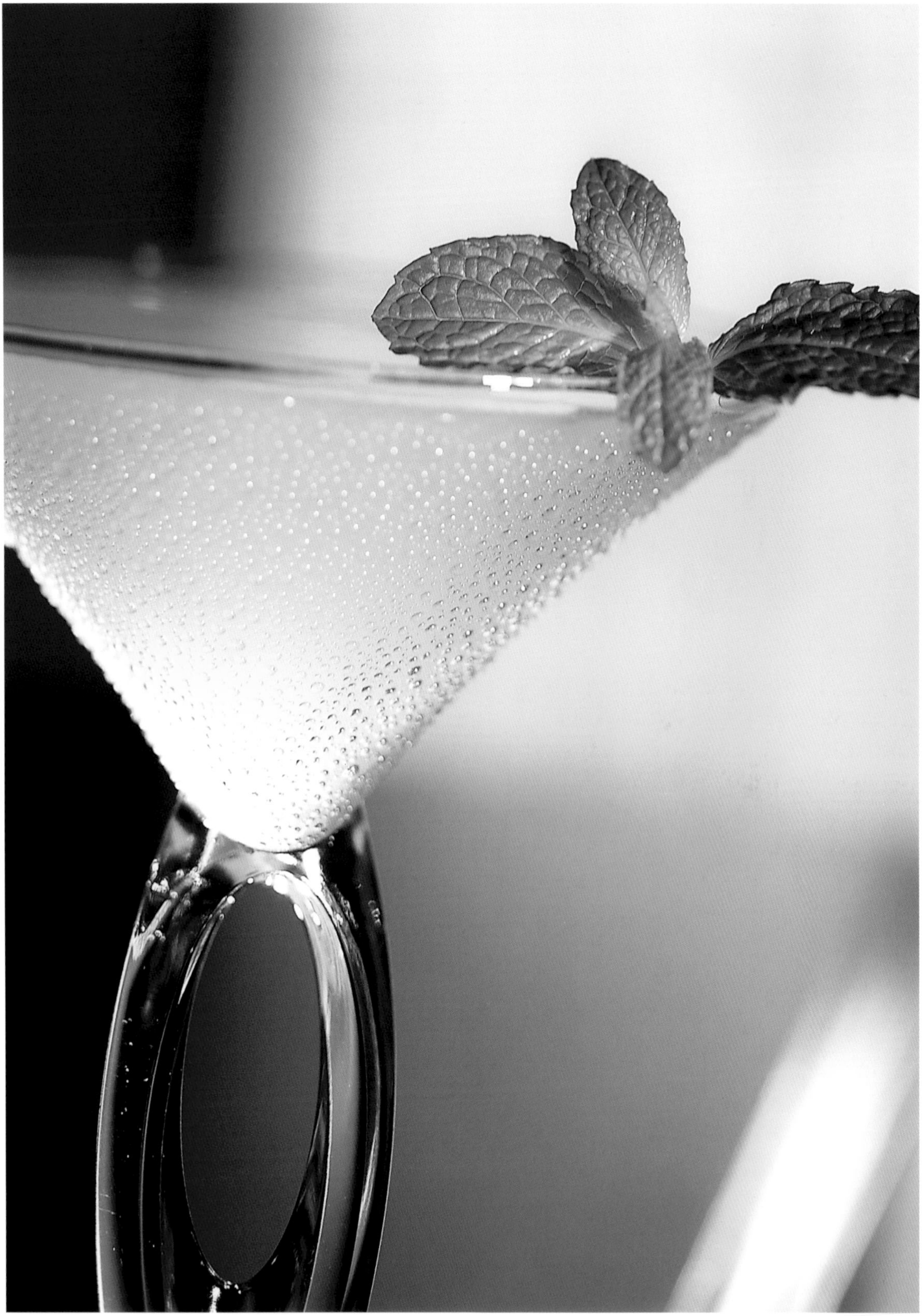

The Vodka International — minted cocktail perfection.

Madison Avenue
3 parts white rum
1 part lime juice
1 part Cointreau
5 mint leaves per glass

Having successfully adjusted the most basic cocktail key, the Daiquiri, it is worth looking at how this technique might affect another one. The infusion of the fragrant mint oils into Cointreau provides a complex contrast of tastes and allows us to develop minted Margarita varieties. There have been some delicious and successful recipes along these lines in the past, such as the white rum variation — the Madison Avenue — but, surprisingly, they have faded into obscurity.

The Madison Avenue, a very old recipe and an apt reminder that perhaps our great grandparents' tastes weren't quite as conservative as we once thought.

Ginger Mojito
5 parts white rum
1 part lime juice
1 $^1/_2$ parts sugar syrup
3 slices ginger per glass
top with soda water

Further experimentation
Although mint is predominantly used in Mojito variations, try looking at how other herbs and flavourings might be incorporated into the Mojito formula. Ginger, for example, is often matched with lime in cooking so, following this reasoning, you can expect them to combine well when muddled together in a cocktail. Sure enough, the Ginger Mojito shows how simple taste combinations can be used to great effect.

The addition of spicy ginger adds a sharp bite to the Mojito.

Basil and Strawberry Mojito
5 parts white rum
1 part lime juice
1 1/2 parts sugar syrup
4 slices strawberry per glass
5 basil leaves per glass
top with soda water

Sometimes the most startling combinations can provide a pleasant surprise. Basil is not a herb that would seem to lend itself naturally to the Mojito recipe, but it can provide an intriguing taste alternative. The Basil and Strawberry Mojito adds the freshness of strawberries to provide a curiously tasty counterpoint to the slightly spicy notes provided by the basil.

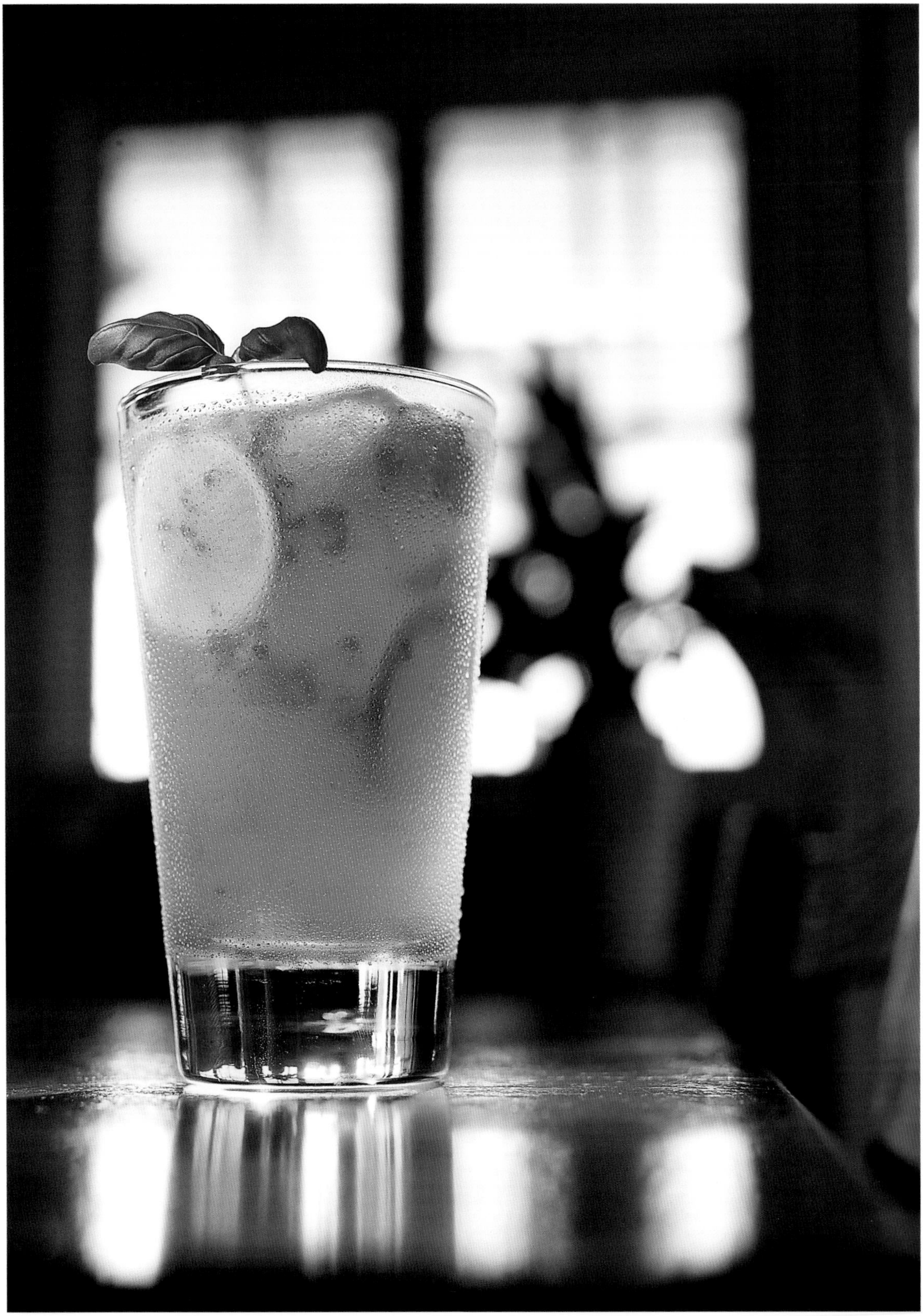

How does something that sounds so wrong taste so right?

Infusions

The point of the Mojito is, of course, to infuse the flavours provided by the mint into your recipe so it can combine with your base spirit. Spirits manufacturers and distillers throughout history have experimented with different varieties of infused spirits, adding the flavours during the distillation process. In recent years, there has been a boom in the number of pre-infused brands available, particularly in the highly competitive vodka market. These brands, ranging from simple lemon infusions to more esoteric varieties such as feijoa, are well worth using as an ingredient in any of your recipes. A great deal of satisfaction, however, can be gained from making your own spirit infusions and making original cocktail recipes that are entirely unique. There are two ways to go about infusing your own spirits — one fast and one slow.

Fast infusions Although most spirits can be used as a base for a fast infusion, the neutral taste of vodka makes it the easiest to use. Simply add the ingredient to the bottle and leave it to sit at room temperature. The time an infusion can take tends to be a matter of trial and error and more delicate tastes, including mint, have little or no effect on vodka's strength. The best results come from using more pungent additions, such as split vanilla pods, which can impart a delicious vanilla aroma to a bottle of vodka usually within a week. Infusions using sweeter ingredients, such as liquorice, are ready as soon as the added material has dissolved.

Infusing lollies (hard candy) can create a sweet and soothing vodka shot.

Slow infusions The slow infusion can take over a year before it has reached the point at which it can be fully enjoyed. To make a slow infusion use dried fruit — such as apricots, apples, pears or figs — or a combination of them, and put them in a large bottle or container that has a tap at its base. Cover the fruit with your chosen spirit, seal the container and get on with your life! Eventually the mixture will achieve a delicious, sticky taste replete with the complexities of your fruit and base spirit ingredients. Simply top up the mixture whenever it is sampled and you will never have to make another batch again.

Like commercially produced infusions, the added flavourings of both fast and slow infusions won't come to the foreground of any recipe unless they are highlighted by an addition of the trusty sweet–sour balance.

Moving on Quite why the Mojito took so long to make the journey from Hemingway's table to mainstream acclaim is anyone's guess, but the strength of that popularity confirms its place among the greatest cocktail recipes.

One drink that has always remained among that select group, indeed it was probably its first member, is the next of our cocktail keys — the Dry Martini.

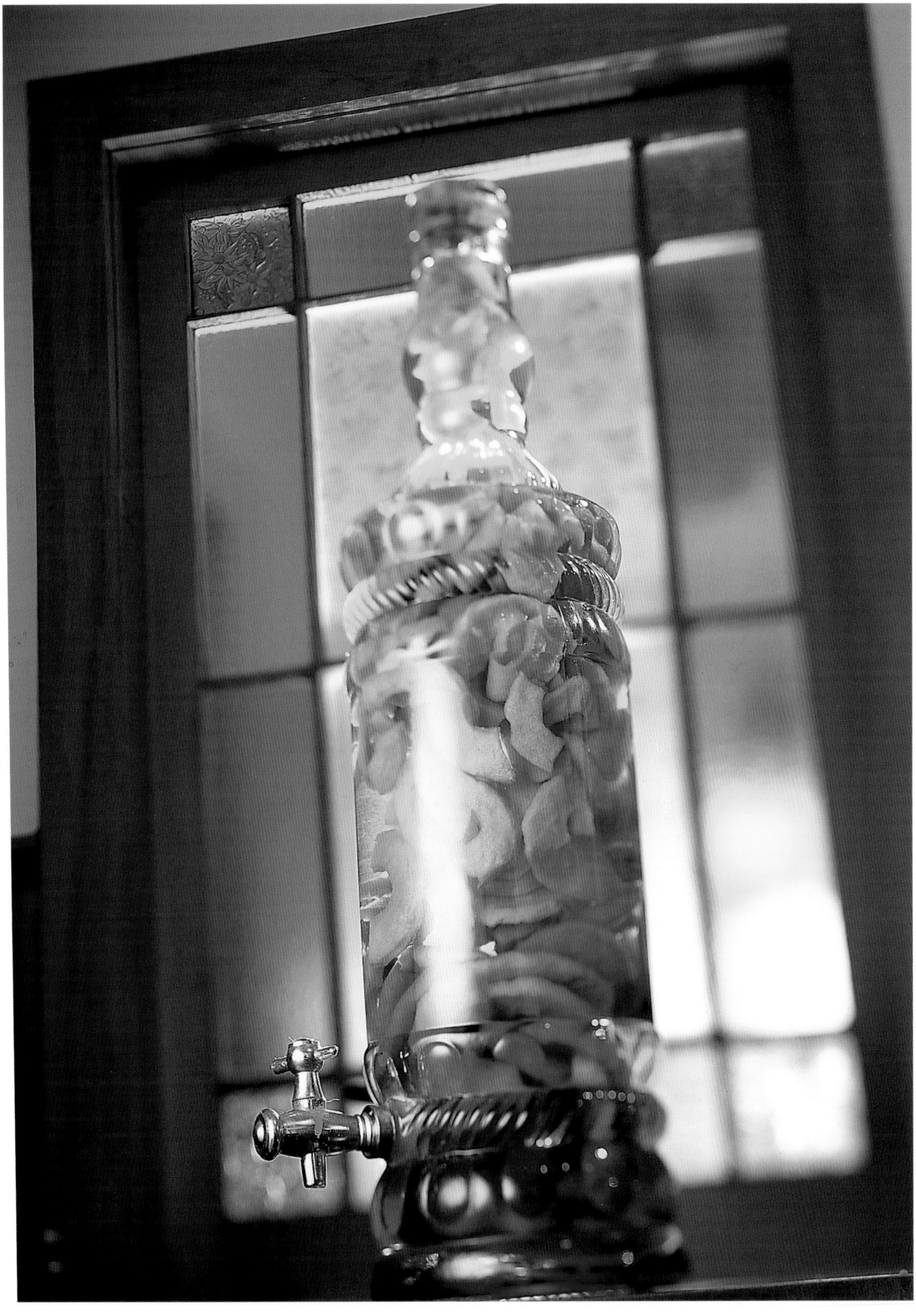

A long, long wait but oh so worth it.

When it comes to the drinks that have inspired cocktail-making folklore, the Dry Martini stands head and shoulders above the competition. But what is a Dry Martini?

If you were to ask a hundred dedicated Martini drinkers that question you would be likely to receive a hundred different answers, such is the aura surrounding this legendary drink. The myths that have sprung up concerning its creation, the thousands of references in literature and music, coupled with James Bond's famous 'shaken, not stirred' tag line, have imbued the 'Silver Bullet' with an ice-cold chic that has ensured its place as an unrivalled liquid cultural icon.

But, for all the fables identifying who mixed the first and the debate over ingredients (that even includes a scientific paper on the subject), the truth is that the Dry Martini is probably the simplest drink to mix of all our cocktail keys. That being said, it's also extremely easy to get wrong, and a bad Dry Martini tends to taste very wrong indeed.

When it comes to the drinks that have inspired cocktail-making folklore, the Dry Martini stands head and shoulders above the competition. But what is a Dry Martini?

If you were to ask a hundred dedicated Martini drinkers that question you would be likely to receive a hundred different answers, such is the aura surrounding this legendary drink. The myths that have sprung up concerning its creation, the thousands of references in literature and music, coupled with James Bond's famous 'shaken, not stirred' tag line, have imbued the 'Silver Bullet' with an ice-cold chic that has ensured its place as an unrivalled liquid cultural icon.

But, for all the fables identifying who mixed the first and the debate over ingredients (that even includes a scientific paper on the subject), the truth is that the Dry Martini is probably the simplest drink to mix of all our cocktail keys. That being said, it's also extremely easy to get wrong, and a bad Dry Martini tends to taste very wrong indeed.

The Dry Martini

The Dry Martini
7 parts gin
1 part dry vermouth

A drink that has been placed on a pedestal throughout cocktail history.

Mixing a Dry Martini

Fill the mixing glass with fresh ice. Add vermouth, stir 20 times and strain into the sink. Pour gin over the ice rinsed in the vermouth and stir a further 20 times. Strain into a well-chilled cocktail glass and garnish.

Technique Setting aside the 'stir versus shake' debate for a moment, let us look at the last of our cocktail-making techniques — stirring. There are three things to bear in mind. Firstly, any drink, and particularly the Dry Martini, should be served at the lowest temperature possible. It is preferable to keep your glasses in the freezer but, failing that, fill them with ice and let them stand until thoroughly chilled. Secondly, the stirring method also adds an often overlooked, and vital, element of the Dry Martini — water. During the stirring process, the water released due to melting will eventually contribute to around a quarter of the volume of your finished Martini and, for this reason, the purity of the ice you are using becomes even more important than usual. Lastly, once you have started mixing a Dry Martini, don't stop! The quickest way to ruin a Dry Martini is to interrupt the mixing process in mid-flow, leaving the finished result hopelessly watery and undrinkable. Make sure you have all the required ingredients and equipment to hand and move fluently from one step to the next.

Your Martini

If you take up drinking Martinis, one day you will no doubt meet the pedantic cocktail purist who will pour scorn on the way you mix your drinks and insist that only they hold the key of creating the perfect Dry Martini. So, in lieu of that conversation, let's get one thing straight — there is only *one* perfect Dry Martini. It is the one that best suits *your* particular tastes. Ignoring the purist's advice, let us now look at the elementary steps to finding the recipe for creating your Dry Martini.

Ingredients Dry vermouth, also known as French vermouth, is a fortified wine flavoured with herbs and spices. Like most fortified wines, once opened, it has a long shelf life and most brands are relatively inexpensive. That cannot be said of the main ingredient. Whether you prefer the traditional gin or more modern vodka, a fairly good rule of thumb when it comes to the resulting cocktail is that you get what you pay for. More than any other drink, the Dry Martini will showcase the subtle alchemy of the distiller's art and the best spirits don't come cheap. Before making an investment, therefore, it might pay to do some research.

'Dry' or 'wet'? A Dry Martini is one that has only has a hint of vermouth in the final mixture. In our base recipe we rinsed the ice with the vermouth, leaving only a tiny fraction to bond with the gin. If you prefer your Martini 'wetter', then add an extra dash with the gin. If you prefer it 'drier', then miss out the vermouth altogether.

Once you have learned how to mix your perfect Martini you may never trust anyone else with the task again.

Vodkatini
7 parts vodka
1 part dry vermouth

Strength There is no escaping the fact that the Dry Martini is a potent drink, after all, that is partly the point of it. Our base recipe produces a good, mid-strength result. If you prefer yours weaker, simply stir longer. If you prefer a stronger mix, leave your gin in the freezer, allowing less ice to melt and lowering the percentage of water in the final cocktail.

Shake or stir? The cocktail purist might point out that when a Dry Martini is shaken, it should actually be called a Bradford and, besides, shaking 'bruises' the gin. However, the Bradford moniker fell out of use decades ago and neither gin nor vodka runs the risk of being 'bruised' in your shaker. Instead, the action of shaking punches air into the mixture, leaving it clouded by thousands of tiny gas bubbles. When the Martini is poured, it is opaque at first and lacks the same crystal-clear quality of the stirred recipe until the air dissipates a couple of minutes later. Despite this, shaking a Martini can often be far less fiddly and time-consuming while still producing a wonderful result. So, whether to shake or stir is really a matter of aesthetics over time economy. The stirred Dry Martini is often visually more attractive, whereas the shaken version can save time and effort and produce a very similar-tasting result.

007's endorsement led to vodka's almost universal acceptance as a substitute for gin.

The Tanqueray Gin Gibson
7 parts Tanqueray gin
1 part dry vermouth
garnish with cocktail onions

Garnish The stuffed green olive has always been the quintessential Martini garnish. The stuffing can vary from the traditional red pimento to more outlandish varieties such as tuna and blue cheese. Olives can also be swapped for onions, small gherkins (pickles) or even pickled green tomatoes.

It is important to bear in mind that the Martini garnish is there for more than just decoration. The olive generates a distinctive burst of pure flavour that cuts across the clean, crisp, iced taste of the Martini, providing a sublime contrast in flavours. Your garnish, then, will make a distinct difference as to how you enjoy your Martini. Unless you wish to tone down the taste contrast and drink your Martini 'dirty', make sure you rinse your choice of garnish thoroughly before adding it to the glass.

The Tanqueray Gin Gibson is the classic Dry Martini recipe offset by the crisp tang of cocktail onions.

The Sweet Martini
4 parts gin
1 part sweet (red) vermouth
garnish with an orange twist

Twist Another alternative to the olive is, of course, the twist. A twist can be made from the zest of any citrus fruit and can serve both decorative and taste purposes. Cocktail bars will often serve Martinis containing beautifully spiralled lemon twists. The problem with those twists is that most of the flavoured citrus oils have often been lost during their creation, so let us take a look at two different versions of the twist — one for decoration and one that provides taste.

To create a twist for decoration, cut a long ribbon of zest from a lemon and tightly wind it around a straw or a chopstick. Slide the twist down the side of your Martini.

To create a twist for taste, slice off a circular section of zest. Holding the zest skin-side-out pinch it between your fingers, spraying the oils across the surface of the drink. Then, wipe the spent zest around the rim of the glass. For extra flavour, leave the zest in the drink.

As a further alternative, the oil from a citrus twist can be ignited, giving a wonderful scorched citrus zestiness to the Dry Martini. The flame must be held at least 10 cm (4 inches) above the Martini's surface, otherwise the oils will not fully combust and will leave a sooty residue on the surface.

The Sweet Martini is made with sweet (red) vermouth. Mix the vermouth with the gin in a ratio of 4:1 and garnish with an orange twist.

The Manhattan
2 parts rye whiskey
1 part sweet (red) vermouth
Angostura bitters, to taste
garnish with cherry

The Manhattan

Before we move on and look at some of the ways to experiment with the Martini, it is worth taking a moment to mention one of its close relatives and another of the cocktail greats — the Manhattan.

Unlike the Martini, there is little disagreement about the Manhattan's origins. In 1874, Jennie Jerome (also remembered as Lady Randolph Churchill, mother of the famous Winston) threw a party for the politician Samuel J. Tilden at the Manhattan Club. The bartender was asked to create something special for the occasion and he named his new concoction the Manhattan after its birthplace. The original recipe has survived to this day owing to the fact it is a sublime way of serving rye whiskey.

Later in its history, the Manhattan subdivided into three separate drinks: the original recipe became known as the Sweet Manhattan; the Dry Manhattan uses dry vermouth; while the Perfect Manhattan has equal measurements of sweet and dry vermouth.

The simple cherry garnish is the distinctive mark of the Manhattan.

Parisian Martini
5 parts gin
1 part crème de cassis

Experimentation

For all its celebrated status as an unrivalled delicacy, caviar is very much an acquired taste and often the palate must be trained before one can begin to enjoy it to the full. The same applies to the Dry Martini — an unprepared palate can be quickly put off by the sheer amount of alcohol overwhelming the taste buds and, until recently, it remained very much an elitist's drink. So, if you find the original somewhat daunting, let's look at how to vary the basic premise in order to make this cocktail more approachable.

New Martinis The 'new Martini' revolution that swept through cocktail bars in the 1990s had two things to thank for its success. Firstly, the Martini name was already firmly established as a symbol of drinking cool. Secondly, by adding sweeter elements to the basic Martini, the daunting alcoholic burn was reduced and the resulting taste had a far more mainstream appeal.

However, this was not a new idea. The Parisian Martini, for example, is a pre-World War II cocktail that calls for the addition of crème de cassis to replace the vermouth in the original Martini recipe. While the liqueur marginally softens the effect of the gin and gives the Parisian a delicate pink hue and a hint of blackcurrant flavour, the drink itself is still relatively overpowering.

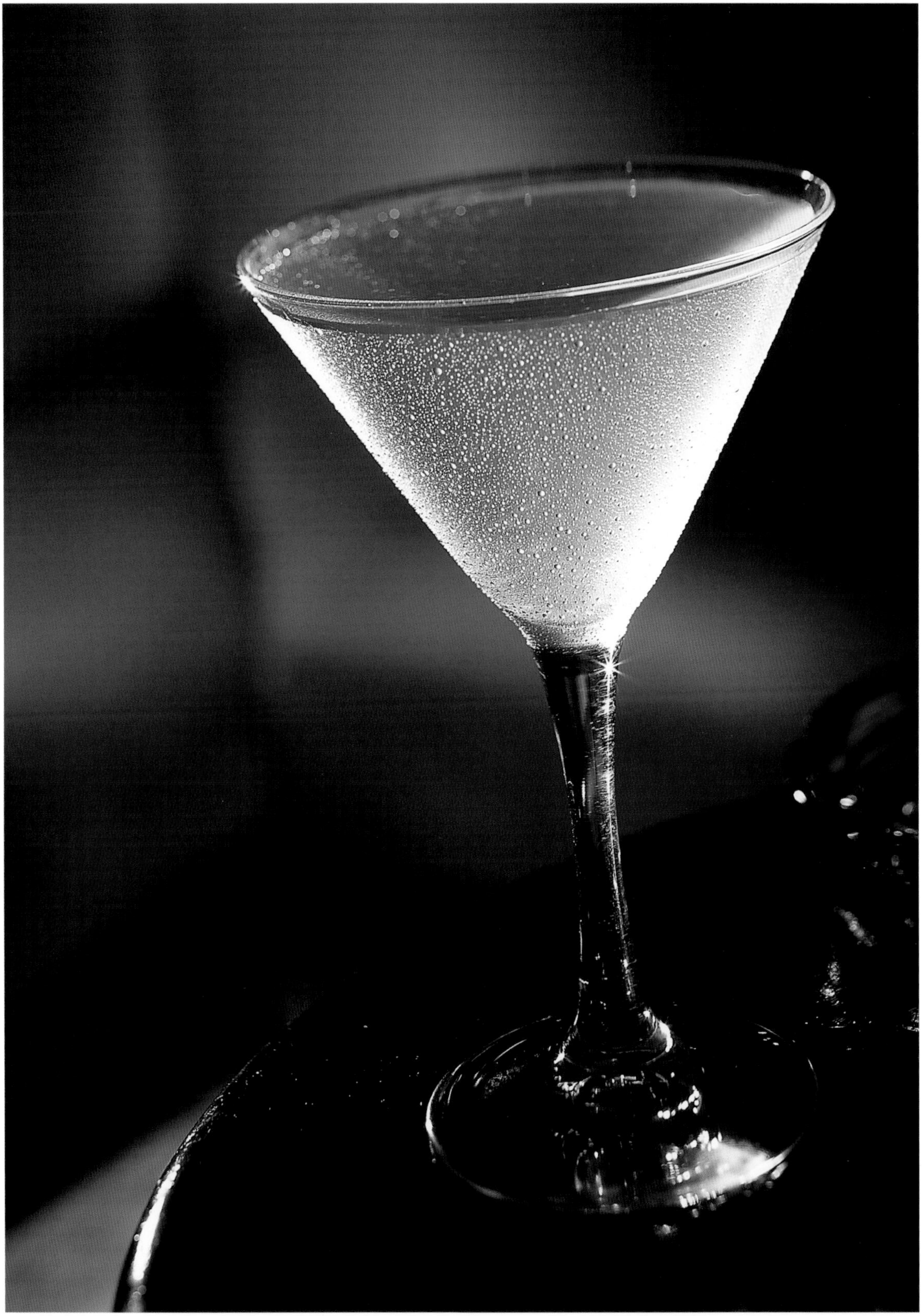

The soft pink tones of the Parisian can be very deceptive!

French Martini
4 parts vodka
1 part crème de cassis
3 parts pineapple juice

If we look at the 'new Martini' vodka equivalent, we can see that the addition of pineapple juice lowers the alcohol content slightly and, more importantly, further sweetens the mixture, rounding off the Parisian's rougher edges. This creates a smooth, palatable alternative while still retaining the Martini's distinctive kick.

Even the most timid of drinkers can enjoy the French Martini.

Cosmopolitan

4 parts vodka
1 part Cointreau
1 part lime juice
1 part cranberry juice
flamed orange twist

Now, let us look at what happens when the sweet–sour elements from our previous cocktail keys are introduced. The heart of the best known of the new Martinis, the Cosmopolitan, relies on the balance familiar to us from the Margarita — Cointreau and lime juice. The recipe is then further softened by the addition of cranberry juice.

Given the variety of juice and liqueurs available, the Cosmopolitan should provide a productive template upon which to base your own designs.

Sex and the City helped, but the classic construction of the Cosmo is the real secret behind its success.

Butterscotch Martini
2 parts vanilla vodka
1 part butterscotch schnapps

It is not necessary to add juice to a Martini to soften the taste of the alcohol. The Butterscotch Martini, for example, balances butterscotch schnapps against a sweeter vodka variant, vanilla, to produce a silky, sweet butterscotch finish.

Notice, though, that the proportions of the butterscotch schnapps — a liqueur with a fairly low alcohol content — have to be fairly high to prevent its effects from being crushed by the greater alcohol yield of the vanilla vodka.

A velvet, butterscotch glove masks the Martini's iron fist.

Mango Martini
3 parts vodka
1 part sugar syrup
3 tablespoons mango flesh, mashed

Fruit Martinis Remembering that a sweetening agent can mute the burn of alcohol, simple sugar syrup can tame a spirit to the extent that additions of fresh or tinned fruit can produce some of the most delicious and refreshing Martini variations.

In the Mango Martini, for example, first mute the vodka by adding sugar syrup at a ratio of about three to one. Then add the mashed mango flesh and shake. This simple formula can be used with a wide range of fruits. When using tinned fruit, a squeeze of lime juice can add a freshness that might otherwise be missing.

A parting word While some might question whether the hallowed Martini name can be applied to anything other than the original creation, the fundamental elements of the recipe can be developed and adjusted to suit almost anyone's taste.

This also applies to our other cocktail keys. These base recipes allow you to explore the cocktail world while following the essential guidelines. The disputes over the origins, recipes and terminology of cocktails pale into insignificance when you are settled in your favourite chair with a well-chilled cocktail in your hand.

Perhaps it is worthwhile to remember that, while it may be a matter of debate who mixed the first Martini, what is really important is . . . who is going to mix the next one?

An innovative way to keep cool during the summer.

Equipment

Glassware

There are literally thousands of shapes and sizes of glassware to choose from. But it is worth considering that most cocktails were designed to fit into one of the four general glass shapes: Martini; old-fashioned; highball; and Champagne flute.

The Martini One of the reasons Martini glasses have their distinctive shape is that cocktails are intended to be served as cold as possible. The characteristically tall stem allows the glass to be held without the warmth of the drinker's hand affecting the temperature of the drink it contains, and prevents condensation from its frigid contents dribbling down and surrounding the glass with a damp patch.

When choosing a Martini glass, ensure it is robust enough to take any punishment, yet elegant enough to remain aesthetically pleasing. It is also important to bear in mind the size of your refrigerator or freezer compartment; chilling your glassware before use is highly recommended and some of the larger varieties on the market may have a hard time cramming themselves into a domestic chiller.

Aim for a middle-sized glass rather than purchasing tiny glasses whose contents will be gone in one gulp, or vessels so huge that the last half of any drink will be lukewarm. A glass with a capacity of between 180–190 ml (6–6½ fl oz) is an excellent choice.

There is nothing that evokes the idea of a cocktail as much as the unique shape of the Martini glass.

The old-fashioned This glass is often referred to as the rocks glass as it tends to be a glass in which drinks are served 'on the rocks'. This will be the most versatile glass in your collection and can be used as the 'mortar' in which to mash limes and sugar to make Caipirinhas or, more simply, to enjoy a single malt whiskey with a couple of lumps of ice.

A larger volume is often required by many recipes served in an old-fashioned so look for a glass at the bigger end of the scale, good and sturdy with a wide, heavy base. A capacity of around 330 ml (11 ¼ fl oz) is an ideal choice.

Your choice of old-fashioned glass should fit your hand comfortably.

The highball This glass lends itself to tall drinks. Look for a variety that will make your creations look elegant and yet still be wide enough to hold ice and garnishes without the drink appearing crowded. A good, basic size to look for, and one that will handle all the requirements of your taller drinks, should have a capacity of at least 350 ml (12 fl oz). Like the old-fashioned, your glass should be sturdy enough to take a fair amount of punishment, as thin-sided highballs are particularly prone to cracking, especially when machine washed.

The slender highball — perfect for your taller drinks.

The Champagne flute This glass was originally developed so the seventeenth-century drinker could enjoy their bubbly while the sediment in those early Champagnes settled at the bottom of the glass. Jean-François de Troy's *The Oyster Lunch*, painted around 1720, depicts a crowd of rowdy bon vivants swilling from flutes; the saucer-like Champagne glasses that seem so traditional to the modern day drinker didn't actually appear until much later.

The Champagne saucer does have a certain retro chic but allows larger amounts of gas to escape from the surface of a sparkling drink and quickly renders its contents flat and lifeless. Today, Champagne saucer glasses are only used as a curiosity, while the flute is the standard and more practical choice in which to serve Champagne and Champagne cocktails.

Like most glasses, Champagne flutes vary in capacity. Look for something tall and elegant with a volume of about 170 ml (5½ fl oz). The weak point of the flute glass is always the stem, so find something relatively sturdy and make sure you hold the body of the glass when polishing, rather than holding the base and twisting.

A flute is the perfect glass for serving deliciously fizzy Champagne cocktails.

Cocktail shakers

Unsurprisingly, the single most important piece of cocktail-making equipment is a cocktail shaker. Simply put, the cocktail shaker is used to thoroughly mix and 'punch' air into a drink while chilling the contents as quickly as possible. There are a multitude of different makes in all manner of sizes and materials, but most shakers conform to two basic types: the 3-piece shaker; and the Boston shaker.

The 3-piece shaker This shaker is most commonly associated with cocktail making and has the advantage of being the easiest to use while delivering excellent results. When shopping for a 3-piece shaker, look for something that fits neatly together without having to be forced. It should make a firm, airtight seal around each section. Cocktails are best shaken individually, so avoid large shakers as the extra volume tends to splinter the ice more readily and water the cocktail down. On the other hand, a shaker that is too small can mean you can't use enough ice to thoroughly chill the drink. A good middle ground is a shaker around the 500 ml (17 fl oz) mark, which will strike a good balance between chilling your concoctions without introducing too much water into the mix.

It is highly recommended that you entirely master the art of using the 3-piece before turning your attention to the other member of the shaker family, the Boston shaker.

While many earlier versions often combined the strainer and body as a 2-piece, the 3-piece shaker proves to be a far more practical and enduring design.

The Boston shaker Many people wonder, given the excellent results produced by the 3-piece shaker and how simple it is to use, why many professional bartenders use a Boston shaker instead. The simple fact is that a Boston shaker, while being more technically difficult to handle, is a great deal more versatile. The glass half of the Boston shaker allows the bartender to keep a visual check on the amount of ingredients being used, as well as serving as a mixing jug for Martinis, the 'mortar' in which to mash Caipirinhas and an extra large highball. When fitted together and used with a bar strainer, the two halves also produce superb shaken cocktails.

There are two problems that can be encountered when first using a Boston shaker. Firstly, the seal between the two cones can become broken while shaking, spraying the contents over unsuspecting guests! To prevent this, make sure you strike the top half of the shaker firmly when fitting it together.

Secondly, having firmly sealed the shaker, it is then impossible to open. This is, frustratingly, a case of practice makes perfect. The idea is to break the seal by striking the centre of the shaker. Don't be tempted to achieve this by thumping it on the edge of a sink or table as this will invariably lead to a broken shaker and a nasty gash on the hand. If the seal won't break, try resting the metal base on a flat surface and applying pressure on the glass half in one direction while patting the seal firmly in the other.

Consisting of two cones — one metal and one glass — the Boston shaker can be adapted to suit a number of cocktail-making techniques.

Mixing jug

The mixing jug is probably the simplest piece of cocktail equipment you will require. While a large glass can easily be used instead, the mixing jug is principally used for stirring Martinis and many choose to invest in a more elegant container in which to mix that fabled concoction. If you wish to add a mixing jug to your equipment, look for a shape designed with those drinks in mind.

The mixing jug provides a stylish vessel in which to stir your Martinis.

Bar blender

By far the most basic way to make cocktails is to throw all the ingredients into a blender and switch it on. However, it is important to remember that all the ice in the blender will then become one of the cocktail's ingredients rather than the means by which the drink is chilled. This often turns even the best designed recipes into nothing better than watered-down, alcoholic slushies.

Despite the garish, outdated blended concoctions of the 1970s, there is still a place for the bar blender in classic cocktail making. The blender can be used to achieve beautiful, delicately balanced drinks while avoiding the temptation to overload a cocktail with surplus liquidized ingredients and unnecessary amounts of ice.

The main requirement to look for in a blender is that it should be powered by a decent motor. There are many domestic blenders on the market but few of them have the power to consistently handle the demands of cocktail making. Although they are more expensive, investing in a top of the range, professional bar blender will guarantee you have a tool specifically designed for the job while ensuring it will almost certainly last for your entire cocktail-making career.

An expensive investment, but a good bar blender should last for years.

Ice

The most fundamental ingredient in making cocktails is ice and while attention is often paid to having the freshest juice, the ripest fruit and the best quality spirits and liqueurs, somehow the quality of the ice is often forgotten.

Only a few domestic water supplies in the world provide delicious water. Most contain a number of unpleasant-tasting chemicals, resulting in ice that can sabotage even your best cocktail-making efforts. A water filter can provide something of a solution to the problem, but bear in mind that cocktail making requires large volumes of ice and instead of making and storing bulky quantities of ice yourself, it may be easier to seek out a local supply. Ice suppliers will generally use filtered water at the very least and will have a fairly neutral taste. Look for bags of ice that contain uniform-sized cubes that have not frozen together into a solid block.

Lastly, strange as it may seem, ice can be too cold! Ice machines used by bars keep their contents at a much higher temperature than those in a domestic freezer. This is because the ice forms a slick, molten layer on its surface, preventing the ice from sticking together and forming large clumps. When using ice straight from the freezer, put your ice in an ice bucket or sink for about half an hour before use and you will find it much easier to handle.

While it may look pure, domestic ice can hide a number of nasty hidden tastes.

Glossary

Absinthe
One of the most notorious spirits in the world, absinthe (a.k.a. The Green Fairy) was banned in France due to the psychoactive properties of one of its ingredients, wormwood. Held responsible by some for a number of drinkers losing their grip on reality and indulging in various unsociable and somewhat gory acts, absinthe was unavailable until the EEC set a limit on the quantity of wormwood permitted in the production process. Modern absinthe is, therefore, somewhat tamer than the original nineteenth-century Parisian version, but is still just as alcoholic. Therefore, anyone wishing to search for the same inspiration as Toulouse-Lautrec should be warned — the alcohol will put paid to you long before *La Fée Verte* does.

Angostura bitters
Angostura bitters was invented in 1824 by Dr J. G. B. Siegert in the Venezuelan town of the same name. Intended as a medicinal tonic, Angostura is made from a recipe containing an aromatic infusion of herbs and spices based on gentian. It is now produced in Trinidad.

Aperitif
An aperitif is a drink taken before a meal with the intention of stimulating the appetite. The term originates from the Latin word, *aperitivus*, meaning 'opener'. Popular aperitifs include the Italian classic Negroni.

Brandy
The term brandy comes from the German *branntwein* meaning 'burnt wine'. Brandy has since become the generic term for distilled grape wine that has not originated from the Cognac region. Brandy is also the base of a number of fruit-flavoured liqueurs such as apricot or cherry brandies.

Cachaça
Cachaça ('ka-shah-sah') hails from Brazil where it is the second most consumed drink after beer (over a billion litres [33 billion fl oz] of cachaça is produced in Brazil every year). The process of making cachaça is similar to rum-making, with one important difference. Instead of using molasses, the cachaça is directly distilled from the fermented juice of the sugar cane.

Most cachaça is filtered instead of aged in oak barrels, although there are some rare and expensive brands that have been aged from 2 to 12 years.

Campari
Campari is a dry, ruby-red Italian bitters laced with herbs and quinine.

Cognac
Approximately 105 kilometres (65 miles) north of Bordeaux, France, on the River Charente lie the towns of Jarnac and Cognac. This is the heart of Cognac-producing country. The soils in this region produce the grapes that make the world's finest brandies — the only ones allowed to be labelled Cognac.

Crème de cassis
Crème de cassis is a sweet, blackcurrant flavoured liqueur.

Crème de fraise
Crème de fraise is a sweet, strawberry flavoured liqueur.

Crème de framboise
Crème de framboise is a sweet, raspberry flavoured liqueur.

Cointreau
Cointreau is a brand of triple sec, a clear orange curaçao, that has become so well known, it is now only referred to by its brand name.

Digestif
Once an integral part of any dinner party, a digestif is a drink taken after the meal and is intended to aid digestion.

Gin
The origin of gin is often traced back to the seventeenth-century Dutch doctor Franciscus Sylvius. While experimenting in the search for an inexpensive diuretic for kidney disorders, he mixed the oil of juniper berries with grain alcohol — both of which were known to have diuretic properties. English soldiers, who were fighting in the Low Countries at the time, were introduced to the relatively inexpensive beverage, which they named 'Dutch courage'. They returned to their homes with a taste for the new drink and shortened the Dutch word for juniper, 'genever', to gin.

Grand Marnier
Grand Marnier is a luscious, Cognac-based liqueur made from the zest of bitter Haitian oranges and blended with spices such as vanilla.

Grenadine
Grenadine is sugar syrup flavoured with pomegranate. The most common varieties are non-alcoholic.

Liqueur

A liqueur is a flavoured alcohol generally used in mixed drinks or, occasionally, on its own as a smaller, sweet drink. Most liqueurs are made by infusing macerated fruit in a base spirit and adding sugar to produce a sweetened alcoholic product.

Méthode champenoise

Like the Cognac area of France, the Champagne region guards its name well — only sparkling wines made in strictly defined regions can be referred to as Champagne. Any other sparkling wines made by the same method in a different part of France, or the rest of the world, are always referred to as méthode champenoise.

Rum

Rum was first produced in the West Indies during the seventeeth century and is the generic term for a distilled sugar-cane spirit. Rum is produced wherever sugar cane grows and the basic process is the same everywhere. Sugar cane is first pressed to release juices that are then boiled down to create a condensed syrup. The sugar within the syrup crystallizes and is removed to leave molasses, which is then used as the base for fermentation.

Rum is produced at various proofs and is generally available in dark or white varieties. The white (or silver) rums are most often used in cocktails as their flavour is much lighter than the darker varieties.

Schnapps

Schnapps is the generic term for a spirit distilled from grain or potato, which is flavoured with fruits or herbs. The infusion can be dry, like vodka, or very sweet and liqueur-like, such as peach and butterscotch schnapps.

Southern Comfort

Southern Comfort falls between being a liqueur and a peach-flavoured whiskey. The base spirit is flavoured with peach extract, fresh peach, orange and herbs. It is said to have derived from a peach and bourbon cocktail.

Sugar syrup

Manufactured sugar syrups have long been used in commercial and home bars as a quick and easy short cut to sweeten drinks without having to wait for sugar crystals to dissolve. Ready-made varieties are most commonly non-alcoholic and are available in many different flavours, with grenadine the most popular choice. Sugar syrup is also simple to create at home (see base recipe on page 16).

Tequila

Tequila is created from the blue mescal, a tall member of the cactus family. At the heart of this plant is a huge pineapple-like fruit known as a pina. The juice of the pina is extracted and left to ferment for up to 5 days, after which the mash is distilled.

Tequila is aged in white oak barrels, with the variety of tequila dictating the style of barrel. For blanco (or silver) tequila, the inside of the barrel is lined with wax to prevent the spirit from extracting colour. An anejo (aged) tequila matures in a normal (unwaxed) barrel so the final product receives a golden tint. A reposado (rested) tequila is a tequila blanco that has undergone a longer maturation process than usual. Gold tequila is usually coloured after the aging process.

Vermouth

Vermouth is a fortified wine flavoured with aromatic roots, herbs, spices and fruit zest. Vermouths were originally created around the foothills of the French and Italian Alps, where each country developed its own unique styles. While both countries now produce both styles, traditional French vermouth was lighter and drier while the Italian varieties were heavier and sweeter.

Vermouth is available sweet or dry. Sweet vermouth is either red (rosso) or white (bianco).

Vodka

It is unclear whether vodka, or wodka, meaning 'little water' originated in Russia or Poland as both were known to be distilling vodka as far back as the twelfth century. There are no strict production guidelines for vodka. Any number of grains (corn, wheat, rye) can be distilled to produce vodka and even potatoes are used to make some eastern European varieties.

The key to quality in vodka lies in the selection of the grain and the purity of the water used. As a general rule, vodka is not aged, to avoid any possibility of inheriting any unwanted characteristics from the cask.

Whiskey

Celtic for 'water of life', whiskey is available in several forms: Scottish malt whiskey is made from spring water and malted barley smoked over a peat fire, matured in oak barrels. Irish whiskey also uses malted barley, but without the smoking process. Rye or Canadian whiskey, is made from rye and other grains such as corn, wheat and barley.

Index

Published in 2005 by Murdoch Books Pty Limited

Murdoch Books Australia
Pier 8/9, 23 Hickson Road, Millers Point NSW 2000
Phone + 61 (0) 2 8220 2000 Fax + 61 (0) 2 8220 2558

Murdoch Books UK Limited
Erico House, 6th Floor North, 93/99 Upper Richmond Road,
Putney, London SW15 2TG
Phone: + 44 (0) 20 8785 5995   Fax: + 44 (0) 20 8785 5985

Chief Executive: Juliet Rogers
Publisher: Kay Scarlett

Design Manager: Vivien Valk
Design Concept and Design: Stephen Smedley
Project Manager and Editor: Paul McNally
Production: Monika Vidovic

National Library of Australia Cataloguing-in-Publication Data:
Cassels, Rob, 1963–. The cocktail keys: the six key classics that
unlock the cocktail kingdom. Includes index. ISBN 1 74045 592 4.
1. Cocktails. 2. Title. 641.874

Printed by Midas Printing (ASIA) Ltd. Printed in China.
Copyright © Murdoch Books 2005
Photography copyright © Todd Antony
Text copyright © Rob Cassels

The author and photographer would like to thank Murray Newby
for the glassware, Sky City Casino, Andy from Crow, Stafford from
Coco Club, and especially Ruthanna Hobday and Chris Lewis.

176